Cooking Rice with an Italian Accent!

Cooking Rice

Other books by Father Giuseppe Orsini
(as Father Joseph Orsini)

ITALIAN FAMILY COOKING: UNLOCKING A TREASURY OF RECIPES AND STORIES

FATHER ORSINI'S ITALIAN KITCHEN

with an Italian Accent!

Father Giuseppe Orsini

THOMAS DUNNE BOOKS
ST. MARTIN'S PRESS ❦ NEW YORK

THOMAS DUNNE BOOKS.
An imprint of St. Martin's Press.

www.stmartins.com

Library of Congress Cataloging-in-Publication Data
Orsini, Giuseppe E.
    Cooking rice with an Italian accent! / Father Giuseppe
Orsini.
        p. cm.
    ISBN 0-312-33902-X
    EAN 978-0-312-33902-9
    1. Cookery (Rice). 2. Risotto. 3. Cookery, Italian. I. Title.
TX809.R5O77 2005
641.6'318—dc22   2004061753

First Edition: September 2005

10 9 8 7 6 5 4 3 2 1

To my Sicilian-Calabrian heritage

*To those people in my life who share my love of God,
my Church, and the meals that I cook*

To my beloved Italy—my earthly Paradise

Contents

ACKNOWLEDGMENTS   ix

FOREWORD BY REGIS PHILBIN   xi

EXPERT ADVICE   xiii

Introduction   1

Getting Ready   5

Common Ingredients and Terms in Italian Cooking   9

Minestre (SOUPS)   13

Risotti (RISOTTOS)   25

Risi (RICE DISHES)   87

Insalate di Riso (RICE SALADS)   133

Dolci (DESSERTS)   139

Epilogue   151

INDEX   153

Acknowledgments

1. MY LORD AND MY GOD — *Who loves me unconditionally. In Him I live, and breathe, and have my being.*

2. ALFREDO SAURINI — *A young man graced with wisdom far beyond his years. He acted as my wine consultant and suggested the appropriate wines to accompany each recipe.*

3. RUTH CAVIN — *My editor, who has taught me how to perfect my writing skills.*

4. JOSEPH RINALDI AND PETER HORAN — *My publicists, who work very hard to make each of my books a success.*

Foreword by Regis Philbin

There is nothing like an Italian who loves to cook, and here is an Italian priest who loves his God, his Church, his family, and the meals he cooks. No kidding, he's the real deal, and incidentally, he loves to eat, too. Maybe it's the blessing he gives the food, maybe it's the collection of great recipes he has saved through the years, or maybe it's because he really loves to cook, but I've been to his table and I can tell you it's an extraordinary dining experience.

But then Father Joe is the kind of guy you love to be with anyway. Such good conversation. Stories you can't make up. Always with a smile. Always up. Always uplifting. I love him.

He has written many cookbooks. This one includes many rice dishes. Who knew rice had such versatility? For me over the years it was white rice or brown rice in Chinese restaurants and I drove the waiter crazy while making up my mind. Father Joe has a million little tips to offer. For example, cauliflower was never my favorite. I never ordered it. Never wanted it. It's lower than Brussels sprouts on my vegetable taste list, but Father Joe gives us a secret about cauliflower. He agrees it's bland, but if you combine it with the right ingredients, it has the ability to absorb other flavors. He has a rice recipe that actually turns the lowly cauliflower into a tempting, tantalizing, taste-pleasing vegetable. Now, if he can do that to a cauliflower, imagine what else he has for you. It's another great book from a great man, a great priest, and a great cook: Father Joe Orsini.

Expert Advice

Who's Afraid of the Big Bad Carb?

You can't read a newspaper or magazine today that does not advocate low carbohydrates or no carbohydrates in the American diet.

As a physician specializing in internal medicine for twenty-five years, I know that the present low carbohydrate fad advocated by some dieticians and some physicians very often is full of confusion and disagreements. This fact compels me to comment about rice and pasta.

In the sports community pasta and rice have been called the foods of champions. These complex carbohydrates are burned off (metabolized) by the body during sports events. Complex carbohydrates are easier to digest than other food sources such as fats and proteins. The body can concentrate more on breaking records rather than converting proteins and fats to energy. Complex carbohydrates such as rice, pasta, whole-grain products, and certain vegetables and fruits lower the glucose response and its effects on insulin. These products keep the energy supply (glucose) moving into the cells at a more constant level with less fluctuation, resulting in less hunger.

Gram for gram pasta and rice are lower in calories than proteins and fats. They also contain B vitamins, riboflavin, niacin, and iron and other nutrients. I personally prepare pasta or rice with simple sauces containing olive oil, garlic, and fresh or canned tomatoes. Depending on the amount ingested it is the sauces heavy with cream, butter, high fat cheese and pork fat that are the culprits in adding additional calories to a dish.

When I desire to lose a few pounds my main meal consists of a 5-ounce serving of pasta or rice with tomato or vegetable sauce. This, of course, must be accompanied by other calorie-restricted meals with low fat content. Vegetables, fruits, whole grains, and low-fat proteins such as fish, chicken, and beans all add to a balanced diet. Of course, if your meal consists of a half loaf of Italian bread, butter, 16 ounces of soda, ½ pound of pasta, or rice with cream sauce, sausage, and chocolate mousse cake, you will find it very difficult to lose or maintain your weight.

The Roman orator Cicero's dictum, "Moderation in all things," also applies to a healthy diet and happier living.

—Don Simone, M.D.

Wine, Companion to Italian Cooking

In the Italian culture, wine is an essential part of a meal, and, needless to say . . . life. Throughout my travels in the wine regions of the world, I have discovered that Italy grows more grape varieties than any other country. I have suggested two wines per each risotto/rice dish. I have been a friend of Father Joe and a big fan of his recipes, and we have shared many glasses of wine with his fabulous dishes. I hope you will experience the same feelings and passion we feel when you sit at the table with friends and family.

Salute,
Alfredo Saurini
Wine Specialist

Cooking Rice with an Italian Accent!

Introduction

In my other cookbooks, I always included rice dishes cooked in the Italian manner. This book is comprised totally of recipes that have rice as a fundamental ingredient.

The majority of these dishes have their origin in Northern Italy because most rice grown in Italy comes from the valley of its major river, the Po. Rice is the pasta of Northern Italy. I will be presenting a number of dishes using rice, everything from soups, salads, main courses, and even a few desserts. I am sure you will be as delighted as I was to discover these many pearls of Italian cuisine that are unknown, at least outside of Italy.

Rice was first introduced to European gastronomy by the Sicilians. In the ninth century, the Arabs brought rice farming to Sicily. Unfortunately, the methods of cultivation in those times were rudimentary and the terrain produced sparse crops. Hence the price was high and rice was served only on the tables of the wealthy. In the centuries following, the situation became progressively worse and the planting of rice in Sicily was completely abandoned.

However, as soon as a tourist arrives in Sicily today, his first encounter with the cuisine will be with rice croquettes called *arancini.* They are sold everywhere, in fry stands on the beach, in cafés, and in bars serving hot food (*tavloa calda*). This is easy to explain. The Sicilians' love of this particular dish remained, even though rice was not readily available.

Be that as it may, this southern Italian concedes that Northern Italy has raised cooking rice to an art.

When I was on *Live! with Regis and Kathy Lee* in 1992, I cooked a risotto Calabrese. I had a tough time explaining to Regis what a risotto was. We wound up shouting at each other, but in jest. To finally clear up any misunderstanding, Regis, here is how a risotto is made: You begin by usually sautéing onions in butter and olive oil. Next, add the rice and sauté that, too. Then you add boiling hot broth, cup by cup, until the rice absorbs all the liquid. This takes about eighteen minutes of continual stirring with a wooden spoon. Okay. Let's go back to the beginning.

In order to better understand Italian cooking, we have to know some basic facts about Italy. Italy is a peninsula shaped like a boot. It is a relatively small country; two-thirds the size of the state of California. Including Sicily and Sardinia, it has only 116,216 square miles.

Being a peninsula means that Italy is surrounded by seas: the Tyrrehenian on the west, the Ionian on the south, and the Adriatic on the east. The rocky Tyrrehenian coast has two principal ports: Genoa and Naples. The Adriatic coast is rich with gorgeous beaches; the Ionian coast is essentially a desert.

At its north, the Alps separate Italy from the rest of Europe. At the feet of the Alps begins the Po valley, a large, flat plateau of very fertile soil. South of this valley there is another chain of mountains, the Appenines, which cross down the middle of the peninsula from north to south. With the exception of the Po valley, Italy is primarily a mountainous country. It is about 750 miles long. The width varies from 395 miles in the Po valley to 25 miles in Calabria.

In the Padana valley we find the principal river of Italy: the Po, which flows from the Alps to the Adriatic Sea. Other important rivers are the Adige, also in the Padana valley, the Arno, which passes through Florence and Pisa; and the Tiber, which flows through Rome. At the foot of the Alps there are the famous beautiful lakes of Como, Maggiore, and Garda.

Italy has two large islands, Sicily and Sardinia, and many small islands, among which are Capri, Ischia, and Elba, all very beautiful and important as centers of tourism. Italy also has three volcanoes: Vesuvius in the gulf of Naples, Etna in Sicily, and Stromboli on the island of the same name.

Italy is situated in a temperate zone, and the Alps protect it from the northern winds, while the surrounding seas make the winters mild. But the climate varies a great deal between the north and south, and even from region to region. In general, winters are cold in the Po valley and in northern and central Italy: but along the Riviera to the east and west of Genoa, winters are mild. Winters are very mild along the Neapolitan and Calabrian coasts and in Sicily. Summers are hot and dry, but very pleasing along the coasts and in the Alps and Appenines.

Italy's north, central, and south are administratively divided into twenty regions, and the regions divided into provinces. Northern Italy comprises the regions of Piedmont, Lombardy, Liguria, Emilia-Romagna, and Veneto. These are agricultural and industrial regions and are very prosperous. Milan and Turin, the two great industrial centers, are in this zone. The regions of Central Italy are: Tuscany, Umbria, The Marches, Lazio, Abruzzi, and Molise. These are essentially agricultural. The South and its regions are also agricultural. Campania is very fertile, and Puglia is also very agriculturally developed. But in the regions of Basilicata and Calabria the level of agriculture is very low because the soil is depleted. Sicily and Sardinia also belong to the South and are also agricultural, because the soil is rich in volcanic minerals.

It is also important to keep in mind that there are two independent countries within Italy's borders: The republic of San Marino and the Vatican City state.

Because of its geography and history, Italy offers the best of many different ethnic groups, diverse languages, and many different styles of cooking. This last is the result of foreign invasions and settlements. There is no such thing as an Italian cuisine per se, rather there are many regional cuisines, making Italian cooking an endless source of variety. When Italy was finally unified into a modern nation in 1870, the great Italian statesman Giuseppe Mazzini proclaimed: *"Abbiamo fatto L' Italia, adesso dobbiamo fare Italiani"* (We have created Italy, now we must create Italians). It hasn't happened yet, but in the meanwhile, Italy has given and continues to give the world one of its most appreciated gifts: Food for humans that is fit for the gods. Because of its great art, architecture, music, philosophical thought, science, foundations of law, systematic theology, and its glorious cuisines, little Italy is a giant among the family of nations.

Now let's get down to some serious cooking, okay?

Getting Ready

Most of these recipes, except for the desserts, of course, require either chicken or beef stock, or broth. I like to make my own stocks and keep them on hand in my freezer. There are times when I run out of my homemade stocks, and I will use canned chicken or beef broths. Swanson is the brand I prefer. I also stock my pantry with Goya chicken and beef bouillon cubes. They are very convenient and make acceptable stocks.

Many of these recipes use Arborio rice imported from Italy. It is a must where indicated. It may be mail-ordered from:

Dean and Deluca's
121 Prince Street
New York, N.Y. 10012

Where long-grain rice is indicated, I prefer Uncle Ben's Converted Rice. Of course, you may choose your own brand. But please, no instant or quick cooking or boil-in-the-bag stuff! Don't even think about it, okay?

Most of these recipes require grated Parmesan cheese which is mild and delicate in taste. Buy it by the piece and grate it freshly yourself. Stay away from grated Parmesan cheese that comes in a cardboard or glass container. It won't do your cooking justice. A few recipes require Pecorino Romano cheese, which is more robust in flavor. My advice for buying and using this cheese is the same as for Parmesan.

Julienne is a cooking term that means to cut the ingredient with a sharp knife so that the slices will resemble matchsticks.

Dice means to cut the ingredient into cubes.

Mince means to chop the ingredient into fine pieces.

Parsley—use only the flat leaf (Italian) variety. It has more flavor.

Herbs—use only fresh herbs unless otherwise indicated.

If you have the time, please use the following recipes for your own homemade stocks.

Brodo di Manzo
(BEEF BROTH)

5 quarts water	4 teaspoons salt
3 pounds boneless beef chunks	2 large onions, unpeeled
3 pounds boneless veal stew chunks	2 celery ribs
2 pounds beef bones	2 large carrots, unpeeled but scrubbed

Rinse all the ingredients (except salt) under cold running water. Place 5 quarts water and the salt in an 8-quart pot. Bring to boil on high heat, then add all the ingredients and return to full boil. After five minutes, reduce heat to low and simmer broth very slowly for two and a half hours. Skim foam from the surface from time to time. Remove the meat, bones, and vegetables from the broth. Strain the broth through a muslin kitchen towel or several layers of cheesecloth lining a colander. Refrigerate overnight and skim any solid fat from the top. Store in plastic containers in the refrigerator for one more day. Skim off any remaining fat. Then store in the freezer for up to three months.

What to do with the meat? Shred it and refrigerate it. You can add quantities of it to your soups or you can make an Italian meat salad by adding chopped celery and onion to the meat and dressing it with salt, pepper, vinegar, and olive oil. The vegetables and bones must be discarded.

Brodo di Pollo

(CHICKEN BROTH)

4 quarts water	2 large onions, unpeeled
1 whole chicken, 3 to 4 pounds	2 celery ribs
1 tablespoon salt	1 large bunch flat leaf parsley

Wash the chicken under cold running water. Place 4 quarts water and the salt in a 6-quart pot. Bring to boil on high heat. Add chicken and vegetables and bring back to full boil for five minutes. Reduce heat to low and simmer for two hours, skimming foam from time to time. Remove chicken with slotted spoon. Strain broth through colander lined with muslin kitchen towel. Refrigerate overnight. Skim off all fat from the top. Freeze in plastic containers for three or more months. Use the chicken meat for chicken salad.

Common Ingredients and Terms in Italian Cooking

Al burro   Dressed with butter

Al dente   Not overcooked; firm-textured pasta

Al forno   Cooked in the oven

All 'aceto   In vinegar

Alla casalinga   Home style

Alla marinara   Seaman style

Arrosto   Roast meat

Asparagi   Asparagus

Baccala   Dried salt cod

Basilico   Sweet basil

Bel Paese   Semi-soft mild cheese

Biscotto   Biscuit

Bistecca   Beefsteak

Braciolo   Meat for rolling and stuffing

Brodo   Broth

Caffè latte   Coffee with milk

Caffè espresso   Black "espresso" coffee

Cannelloni   Large round pasta often served stuffed

Capperi   Capers

Carciofo   Artichoke

Cassata   Rich cake

Cavolfiore   Cauliflower

Cavolo   Cabbage

Cipolla   Onion

Coppa   Cup

Costoletta   Cutlet

Crudo   Raw or uncooked

Ditali   Short tubular pasta

Ditallini   A small variety of the above

Dolce   General term for dessert

Fagioli   Dried beans

Fagiolini   Fresh beans

Farina bianca   White wheat flour

Farina integrale   whole-wheat flour

Fegato   Liver

Fettucine   Homemade narrow ribbon pasta

Filetto   Thin fillet of meat or fish

Finocchio   Fennel

Formaggio   Cheese

Frittata   Omelet

Frittelle   Pancakes; term also used for fritters

Fritto misto   Mixture of fried foods

Frutti di mare   Small shellfish

Funghi   Mushrooms

Gàmberi   Shrimp

Gelato   Frozen—usually ice cream

Imbottiti   Stuffed

Involtini   Slice of meat stuffed and rolled

Insalata   Salad

Lasagne   Wide flat noodles

Latte   Milk

Lesso   Boiled

Limone   Lemon

Maccheroni   Macaroni; a generic term for all types of pasta

Maiale   Pork

Manzo   Beef

Melanzane   Eggplant

Minestra   Soup; also generic term for pasta or rice course

Minestrone   Thick vegetable soup

Mozzarella   A soft white unsalted cheese

Olio   Oil

Oliva   Olive

Origano   Herb used for flavoring: Oregano

Pane   Bread

Pane abbrustolito   Toasted bread

Panna   Cream

Parmigiano   Hard cheese much used in Italian cookery: Parmesan

Pasta   Dough; generic term for all macaroni products

Pasta asciutta   Pasta served with butter or a meatless sauce

Pasta in brodo   Pasta cooked in broth and served as soup

Pasta secca   Eggless pasta

Pasta all'uovo   Egg pasta

Pasta verde   Green (spinach) pasta

Pasticceria   General term for pastry

Pastini   Small pasta shapes used in soup

Pecorino   Strong sheep's milk cheese

Peperóne   Sweet peppers

Peperoncini   Small hot peppers

Pesce   Fish

Pignoli   Pine nuts

Polenta   Cornmeal mush

Pollo   Chicken

Polpette   Small meatballs

Polpettone   Large meat loaf

Pomodoro   Tomato

Prezzémolo   Parsley

Prosciutto   Ham

Provolone   A hard yellow cheese

Ravioli   Stuffed squares of pasta

Ricotta   Soft curd cheese, "pot cheese"

Rigatoni   Large grooved macaroni

Ripieno   Stuffed or stuffing

Riso   Rice

Risotto   Rice dish

Salsa   Sauce

Salsiccia   Generic term for sausage

Scaloppine   Thin small slices of veal or breast of chicken

Scampi   Large shrimp

Sedano   Celery

Spaghetti   Long, thin varieties of pasta

Spinaci   Spinach

Spumante   Sparkling wine

Sugo   Sauce

Tagliatelle   Homemade ribbon pasta

Tonno   Tuna fish

Torrone   A type of nougat candy

Torta   Generic term for cake

Tortellini   A stuffed pasta

Trippa   Tripe

Uovo   Egg

Uva   Grapes

Verdure   Vegetables

Vermicelli   Very thin spaghetti

Vino   Wine

Vitello   Veal

Vongole   Clams

Ziti   Tubular-shaped pasta

Zucchini   Squash

Zuppa   Soup

Minestre (Soups)

At an ordinary Italian dinner, soup is the usual first course, followed by a main course of meat, fish, or poultry. Dinner is usually served around two o'clock in the afternoon. About 4 P.M. everyone returns to work. Supper is eaten in the late evening. Often, the only course served is one of the following soups.

Minestra di Riso con Lattuga e Piselli

(RICE SOUP WITH LETTUCE AND PEAS)

SERVES 4

This is a delicate soup with intriguing flavor. It takes about one hour to make and it seems to taste better if made the night before, refrigerated, and reheated for supper. It also has great eye appeal.

3 tablespoons unsalted butter

2 small onions, peeled and thinly sliced

1 small head romaine lettuce, washed and chopped coarsely

9 ounces frozen, shelled, peas

1½ beef bouillon cubes, crushed

1½ quarts water

1½ cups rice (any long-grain rice can be used)

Pinch of salt (⅛ teaspoon)

5 leaves fresh basil, chopped

¼ cup fresh flat leaf parsley, chopped

4 tablespoons half-and-half or light cream

4 tablespoons freshly grated Parmesan cheese

In a large (6-quart) saucepan, sauté the onions for five minutes in melted butter. Add the lettuce and peas. Cook uncovered for ten minutes on moderate heat. Add the bouillon and pinch of salt. Add the water and bring to boil. When the water is boiling, add the rice and cook on simmer for fifteen minutes, stirring often. Add the basil, parsley, cream, and grated cheese. Stir well. Pour into a preheated soup tureen and bring to table.

RECOMMENDED WINES:

LUGANA DEL VENETO, TREBBIANO/MALVASIA BLEND

Minestra Delicata di Riso
(DELICATE RICE SOUP)

SERVES 4

Legendary Verona is the location of Shakespeare's tragic play, Romeo and Juliet. *At its center is a Roman amphitheater that has been in constant use for over two thousand years. It has a lively and lovely open-air market, near which I first tasted this delicate and beautiful rice soup*

1 tablespoon butter

1 medium white onion, thinly sliced

2 small heads romaine lettuce, outer
  leaves removed (save for salad)
  leaving only the white tender
  hearts, washed, dried, and torn
  into small pieces

1 large potato, peeled and diced
  small

10-ounce package frozen peas,
  completely thawed

2 quarts boiling hot chicken
  stock

1 cup long-grain rice

2 tablespoons dry white wine

1 heaping tablespoon freshly grated
  Parmesan cheese

1 tablespoon flat leaf parsley,
  chopped

Salt and pepper to taste

Grated cheese for the table (either
  Parmesan or Pecorino)

In a large saucepan, sauté onion in butter on gentle heat for five minutes. Add lettuce and sauté five more minutes. Add diced potatoes. Stir with wooden spoon. Add peas. Cook for three minutes. Add hot stock. Simmer on low heat uncovered for twenty-five minutes. Add rice, stir, and simmer for eighteen minutes. Add wine, grated cheese, and parsley. Season with salt and pepper. Stir well. Pour into a tureen and bring to the table. Provide more grated cheese to pass at table. *Ottimo!* (The best!)

RECOMMENDED WINES:

BIANCO DI CUSTOZA, SOAVE

Minestra di Riso con Fegatini di Pollo

(RICE SOUP WITH CHICKEN LIVERS)

SERVES 4

Chicken livers have a mild, pleasant flavor in this robust soup. (Have you noticed that you have to buy chicken livers separately these days? I mean separate from the whole chicken. What used to get thrown to the family cat in the old days, now we get to pay a premium price.) This is an earnest soup that I'm sure you'll all enjoy. If the kids ask what the meat is in the soup, tell them chicken. That's not a lie. The livers did come from chickens.

½ large onion, thinly sliced
1 bunch fresh flat leaf parsley, chopped
1 tablespoon olive oil
1 tablespoon butter
3½ ounces dried porcini mushrooms, rehydrated and minced

3½ ounces chicken livers, chopped coarsely
Salt and pepper to taste
1 tablespoon dry white wine
½ cup any long-grain rice
1½ quarts beef stock
Grated Parmesan cheese to pass at table

Sauté the onion and parsley in oil and butter in a large saucepan on low heat for five minutes. Add mushrooms and cook five minutes. Add chicken livers and stir well. Season with salt and pepper. Add wine and cook until it evaporates. Add rice, stir well. Add all the broth. Bring to boil, lower to simmer and cook for fifteen minutes. Serve the soup very hot and pass the grated cheese at table.

RECOMMENDED WINES:

DOLCETTO D'ASTI, LAMBRUSCO DI GRASPAROSSA

Minestra di Riso
con Cavolo Rosso

(RICE SOUP WITH RED CABBAGE)

SERVES 4

This is another hearty soup from the extreme north of Italy on the Austrian border. It is a soup that would be spoiled with the addition of grated cheese. I asked for grated cheese and was told "Absolutely not!" Red cabbage is also very good in a salad and makes an excellent sauerkraut.

1 tablespoon olive oil	2 tablespoons tomato paste, dissolved
1½ ounces pancetta or bacon, minced	in ½ cup dry white wine
2 medium onions, finely chopped	1½ quarts boiling hot chicken or
1 small red cabbage, cut in half and	beef broth
julienned	½ cup long-grain rice
2 large peeled potatoes, diced small	Salt and pepper to taste

Heat oil in a large saucepan on moderate heat, and sauté the pancetta and the onions for eight minutes. Add cabbage and stir for five minutes. Add tomato paste dissolved in wine. Add all the boiling hot broth. Adjust heat to low and simmer covered for one hour. Stir in rice and cook covered for fifteen minutes. Season with salt and pepper. Pour into tureen and bring to table. Genuine rye bread and a glass of beer make this a great meal.

RECOMMENDED WINES:

REFOSCO, SCHIOPETTINO

Crema di Riso e Zucca

(CREAM OF RICE AND PUMPKIN SOUP)

SERVES 4

This is an unusual and enticing first course to put on your Thanksgiving table. It goes well with the roasted turkey and all the other trimmings. It will get rave reviews from your family and guests.

½ large onion, minced

3 tablespoons olive oil

1 can of unflavored pumpkin puree

1 quart boiling hot chicken stock

1 beef bouillon cube dissolved in
  ½ cup hot water

10 ounces long-grain rice

1 tablespoon chopped fresh flat leaf
  parsley

1 tablespoon sugar

5 tablespoons grated Parmesan
  cheese

Sauté onion in olive oil in a large saucepan. Cook on gentle heat five minutes. Add pumpkin and hot stock. Mix well and cook on gentle heat for ten minutes. Add the dissolved bouillon, bring to a boil. Add rice and parsley, and cook for fifteen minutes. Add sugar and stir. Sprinkle with 1 tablespoon grated cheese. Empty into soup tureen, sprinkle with remaining cheese, and serve.

RECOMMENDED WINES:

TOCAI FRIULANO, PINOT BIANCO

Minestra di Riso con Broccoletti

(RICE SOUP WITH BROCCOLI FLORETS)

SERVES 4

Remember what the medical profession is saying about the cancer preventatives found in the cruciferous vegetables, especially broccoli. This soup is a delightful way of enjoying broccoli and is perfect for a cold winter night's supper.

1 medium onion, peeled and diced

1 large clove garlic, peeled and crushed

4 tablespoons butter

1 bunch of broccoli, florets only

Salt and pepper to taste

1 tablespoon tomato paste

1½ quarts boiling hot chicken broth

1 cup long-grain rice

4 tablespoons grated Parmesan cheese

Sauté onion and garlic in 2 tablespoons butter in a large saucepan on gentle heat for five minutes. Add broccoli and stir-fry for five minutes. Season with salt and pepper. Add the tomato paste dissolved in a cup of broth. Stir and cook for ten minutes. Add remaining broth, bring to boil, adjust heat to simmer, and cook for twenty minutes. Add rice, stir, and cook for twenty more minutes. Stir. Add 2 tablespoons butter and grated cheese. Stir and serve. Excellent!

RECOMMENDED WINES:

CHARDONNAY DELL'UMBRIA, MERLOT DI APRILIA

Minestra di Riso e Fagiolini

(RICE AND GREEN BEAN SOUP)

SERVES 4

When I visited Parma, I stayed in one of the most beautiful hotels I've ever seen. It was the Baglioni Palace Hotel (five stars). I could hardly believe its sumptuous luxury. But it made me yearn for simplicity, so I walked through the beautiful city of Parma, stopped at the church of Santa Maria Stecchata, and thanked God for allowing me to be there. Then I meandered through the open-air food market and nearby found a simple family-owned restaurant (trattoria). My yearning for simplicity was satisfied as I sampled this flavorful dish.

2 tablespoons butter	1 large egg
1 medium onion peeled and thinly sliced	Juice of ½ fresh lemon
6 ounces tender green beans, washed and cut into ½-inch pieces	Pinch of salt
	½ teaspoon black pepper
4 large potatoes, peeled and diced small	1 tablespoon chopped fresh flat leaf parsley
1½-quarts water	2 heaping tablespoons grated Parmesan cheese
2 beef bouillon cubes, crushed	2 tablespoons light cream
1 cup long-grain rice	

Melt butter in a large saucepan on moderate heat. Sauté onion for five minutes. Add green beans. Adjust heat to low and sauté for eight minutes. Add potatoes and sauté another eight minutes. Add water and bouillon. Bring to boil. Adjust heat to low and simmer covered for forty minutes. Add rice and cook covered another twenty minutes.

Meanwhile, in a soup tureen beat together the egg, lemon juice, parsley, light cream, Parmesan cheese, and salt and pepper.

When soup is done, whisk egg mixture for one minute and pour into soup in the tureen. Add cream, stir briskly, and bring to table.

RECOMMENDED WINES:

ALBANA DI ROMAGNA, SAUVIGNON BLANC

Minestra di Riso, Rape, e Porri

(RICE, TURNIP, AND LEEK SOUP)

SERVES 4

The broccoli di rape *in the Risotto con Verdure Miste on page 45 is a close cousin to the turnip. In fact, the seeds of* broccoli di rape *are cold-pressed to produce canola oil, an excellent cholesterol-free cooking oil. (It is called Puritan oil in the United States.) This hearty soup is chock-full of turnips, leeks, onion, and potatoes. It is a vegetarian's dream come true. And it tastes terrific!*

2 tablespoons butter

1 medium onion, minced

3 small turnips, peeled and diced

5 leeks, white bulbs only, trimmed of roots, quartered and washed under cold running water several times, then thinly sliced

2 medium potatoes, peeled and diced

Salt and pepper to taste

2 quarts boiling hot chicken stock

½ cup long-grain rice

½ cup chopped fresh flat leaf parsley

2 heaping tablespoons freshly grated Parmesan cheese

In a large saucepan, sauté onion, turnips, leeks, and potatoes in butter on gentle heat for ten minutes, stirring occasionally. Season with salt and pepper. Add all the hot chicken stock, cover, and cook on simmer for twenty minutes. Add rice, stir, and cook covered for another twenty minutes. Remove from heat. Stir in parsley and grated cheese. Pour into a tureen and bring to table. If the dinner guests ask for more grated cheese, for goodness sake, give it to them. You want your guests to be happy, don't you?

RECOMMENDED WINES:

SYLVANER, TOCAI FRIULANO

Minestra di Riso con Spinaci e Uova
(RICE SOUP WITH SPINACH AND EGGS)

SERVES 4

I *am sure we all remember that kids usually detested spinach. Then along came Popeye, the likable little sailor who beat all the odds against him whenever he ate his spinach. I remember when I was in the seminary, canned spinach was often served in the refectory (dinning hall). It looked like seaweed and tasted like the tin can it came out of. One day, my mama made this spinach and rice soup. It has the magical quality of changing spinach haters into spinach lovers.*

2 tablespoons olive oil (the real stuff, not Popeye's girlfriend)

1 large clove peeled garlic, left whole

1 20-ounce package frozen spinach, cooked to package directions, cooled and almost squeezed dry

1 quart boiling hot chicken broth

1 cup long-grain rice

1 large egg

2 heaping tablespoons grated Parmesan cheese

½ teaspoon freshly ground black pepper

In a large saucepan, heat olive oil on moderate heat. Add the whole clove of garlic and sauté until golden brown. Discard garlic. Add spinach, stir. Add hot broth. Add rice, stir, and bring to boil. Cook covered for fifteen minutes. Meantime, beat the egg with the grated cheese in a soup tureen. Pour soup into the tureen and stir vigorously to cook the egg. Bring to table and have more grated Parmesan to pass around.

RECOMMENDED WINES:

PINOT GRIGIO, BARDOLINO

Risi e Bisi

(RICE AND PEA SOUP)

SERVES 6

This recipe comes from Fulvia Sessani, of Venice, Italy. I met Fulvia in Seattle when I was there to do a show with Jeff Smith, The Frugal Gourmet. *She is a charming lady who gave me permission to use her rice recipe in my next book. This Risi e Bisi is a light and delicate rice dish common to the Veneto, the region whose capital is Venice.*

1 ounce butter	6 cups boiling hot chicken stock
3 ounces pancetta (Italian bacon), diced	2 cups shelled peas, fresh or frozen
5 ounces Arborio rice	1 pinch fennel seeds (⅛ teaspoon)
1 small onion, peeled and thinly sliced	4 tablespoons butter
	¼ cup grated Parmesan cheese

In a saucepan heat the one ounce of butter, add the pancetta. Add the rice and onion. Cook, stirring for five minutes. Add hot broth, cup by cup, until rice absorbs all the broth. Stir in peas. Add the fennel seeds. Stir. Remove from heat and add four more tablespoons of butter and the cheese. Stir vigorously. Provide more grated Parmesan cheese at table.

RECOMMENDED WINES:

SOAVE, TOCAI

Riso e Zucca al Profumo di Noce Moscata
(RICE AND PUMPKIN SOUP PERFUMED WITH NUTMEG)

SERVES 4

Zucca *is the Italian word for pumpkin, but in slang it means "dumb jerk." If anyone in Italy calls you* zucca *he won't be trying to sell you pumpkin. This dish is a savory, thick soup that can be served as a main course. I sampled this dish at an Italian fast-food restaurant in the Galeria di Milano, the first indoor shopping mall in the world. It is a jewel of architecture decorated with fine mosaics. After this dining experience, I dropped in to say a prayer at Il Duomo di Milano (Milan's gorgeous gothic cathedral) and thanked God for all He has given me. No one called me* zucca.

3 scallions, washed, trimmed and
    sliced thinly
1 tablespoon butter
3 tablespoons olive oil
1 can of unflavored pumpkin puree

1 quart boiling hot chicken stock
1 cup long-grain rice
3 tablespoons grated Parmesan cheese
A generous pinch of nutmeg
    (¼ teaspoon)

In a large saucepan, place butter and oil and on low heat, sauté the scallions for eight minutes. Add the pumpkin, hot chicken stock, and rice. Mix well, cover and cook on the lowest heat for ten minutes. Remove from heat, sprinkle grated cheese and nutmeg. Stir briskly. Pour into tureen and bring to table. Have salt and pepper and more grated Parmesan cheese on the table for each to season his or her bowl.

RECOMMENDED WINES:

DOLCETTO D'ALBA, BARBERA D'ASTI

Risotti (Risottos)

Risotto is a main course at an Italian dinner (*pranzo*) or supper (*cena*). Basically, a risotto is cooked thus. Onion or garlic is sautéed in butter and/or olive oil. Then the rice is sautéed for three minutes. Other ingredients are added, after which either chicken or beef broth, heated to a boil, is added cup by cup, constantly stirring, until the rice absorbs all the liquid. This takes about eighteen minutes. Arborio rice imported from Italy must be used because it has the ability to absorb much liquid and to become creamy in consistency but still remain al dente (firm to the bite).

Risotto Saporito al Gorgonzola
(FLAVORFUL GORGONZOLA CHEESE RISOTTO)

SERVES 4

I *will not go into a treatise on the pungent, mouthwatering, and hearty aspects of Gorgonzola cheese. Suffice it to say that the recipe takes full advantage of all the virtues of this precious cheese. Gorgonzola has an adult, full flavor; but I've seen Italian kids spreading it on toasted bread for an afterschool snack.*

1 small onion, minced	Salt and pepper to taste
2 tablespoons butter	1 quart boiling hot beef stock
2 tablespoons olive oil	5 ounces Gorgonzola cheese
1½ cups Arborio rice	3 tablespoons light cream
2 tablespoons dry white wine	2 large tablespoons grated Parmesan
(I use Pinot Grigio)	cheese

Sauté onion in one tablespoon of butter and olive oil in a large saucepan on moderate heat for five minutes. Add rice, stir for two minutes. Add wine and cook until it evaporates. Season with salt and pepper. Now add hot beef stock, cup by cup, constantly stirring until all broth is absorbed by the rice (about eighteen minutes). Place Gorgonzola and remaining butter in bowl of food processor fitted with a steel blade and process for one minute. Remove the saucepan from the stove, incorporate the cream, the food-processed cheese and butter, and the grated cheese. Mix well. Let rest two minutes, then serve.

RECOMMENDED WINES:

GATTINARA, NEBBIOLO D'ALBA

Risotto alla Cavour

(CAVOUR'S RISOTTO)

SERVES 4

Camillo Cavour was a prime mover in the movement for the unification of Italy as a modern nation. He, along with Mazzini and Garibaldi, finally freed the Italian peninsula from foreign domination and Italy became a nation under its first king, Victor Emmanuel II of Savoy. This flavorful risotto is named in honor of Camillo Cavour.

1 cup chopped flat leaf parsley

1 large peeled clove garlic, crushed

1 6½-ounce can of tuna packed in olive oil, flaked (use the drained oil to sauté the other ingredients)

2 ribs celery, diced small

1 tablespoon white wine vinegar

1 tablespoon tomato paste, dissolved in ½ cup dry white wine (I use either Pinot Grigio or dry vermouth)

1½ cups Arborio rice

1 quart boiling hot chicken stock

Salt and pepper to taste

1 tablespoon butter

In a large saucepan on gentle heat, sauté parsley, garlic, tuna, and celery in oil from can of tuna for eight minutes. Add vinegar, cook for three minutes. Add tomato paste dissolved in wine and, constantly stirring, cook until wine evaporates. Stir in rice. Add hot stock, cup by cup, constantly, stirring, until rice absorbs all the liquid (about eighteen minutes). Season with salt and pepper. Remove from heat. Stir in butter. Cover and let rest for two minutes. Serve immediately. (No grated cheese, please.)

RECOMMENDED WINES:

ARNEIS, RIBOLLA GIALLA

Risotto alla Rustica
(PEASANT LADY'S RISOTTO)

SERVES 4

This very simple and tasty risotto probably got its name from the fact that farmworkers in Italy, even to this day, always cultivate their own little gardens from which they harvest their own fresh crops. Wouldn't it be wonderful if you could grow your own scallions, garlic, rosemary, marjoram, parsley, basil, and tomatoes? Your cooking would take on a fresher more genuine flavor. However, our truck farms do a very suitable job supplying us with what we need to cook superbly. I like New Jersey–grown veggies, after all, I am a New Jerseyan.

1 large scallion

1 clove garlic, peeled

1 fresh rosemary sprig, leaves only

1 small bunch flat leaf parsley

6 fresh basil leaves

Pinch dried marjoram (⅛ teaspoon)

1½ cups Arborio rice

½ cup dry white wine or
   dry vermouth

4 fresh small tomatoes, peeled and
   squeezed through your fingers

1 quart boiling hot chicken stock

Salt and pepper to taste

2 tablespoons butter

2 tablespoons light cream

2 tablespoons grated Parmesan
   cheese

Wash the scallion, rosemary, parsley, and basil. Dry with paper towel. Mince the fresh vegetables along with the garlic. Melt one tablespoon of butter in olive oil on gentle heat in a large saucepan. Sauté the aromatic mince and marjoram for five minutes. Add rice and stir for three minutes. Add wine and cook until it evaporates. Add crushed tomatoes. Cook eight minutes. Add hot chicken broth, cup by cup, until rice absorbs all the liquid (about eighteen minutes). Season with salt and pepper. During the last two minutes of cooking rice, add 1 tablespoon butter, cream, and grated cheese. Transfer to warmed serving bowl and bring to table. You may want to provide more grated cheese to pass separately.

RECOMMENDED WINES:

PINOT GRIGIO, GEWÜRZTRAMINER

Risotto Giallo con Peperoni

(YELLOW RISOTTO WITH PEPPERS)

SERVES 4

Saffron is a very strong seasoning that has been used in the culinary arts for centuries. Saffron is the dried stigma of the blossoms of Crocus sativus, *a plant native to Asia Minor and grown widely in Europe. Each of the tiny stigmas must be gathered by hand and it takes thousands to make an ounce. This explains why it is the most costly spice in the world. However, a little pinch will permeate a dish with its lovely, strong scent and give it a beautiful yellow color. I had this wonderful risotto while visiting Stresa, a jewel of a village on the shore of Lake Maggiore at the feet of the towering Alps.*

1 tablespoon butter	1 quart boiling hot chicken stock
2 tablespoons olive oil	(reserve 2 tablespoons)
1 large onion, thinly sliced	1 small package saffron (Badia brand,
1 large clove garlic, minced	0.008 gram)
1 green bell pepper, seeded and	10 pitted, ripe black olives, cut into
julienned	rings
1 yellow bell pepper, seeded and	2 tablespoons flat leaf parsley,
julienned	chopped
Salt and pepper to taste	12 fresh basil leaves, torn into pieces
1½ cups Arborio rice	2 tablespoons grated Parmesan
½ cup dry white wine	cheese

Melt butter in oil in a large saucepan on gentle heat. Sauté onion and garlic eight minutes. Add julienned green and yellow bell peppers. Season with salt and pepper. Cook for five minutes. Add rice. Stir three minutes. Add wine and adjust heat to low. Add boiling hot broth, cup by cup, stirring constantly, until rice absorbs all the liquid (about eighteen minutes). During last five minutes of cooking, add black olive rings and saffron dissolved in two tablespoons reserved hot broth. Remove from heat. Stir in chopped fresh herbs. Sprinkle with grated cheese. Stir vigorously. Transfer to serving bowl and bring to table. *Squisito!* (Exquisite!)

RECOMMENDED WINES:

BARBARESCO, MEDIUM-BODIED AGLIANICO

Risotto con Peperoni e Melanzane

(RED BELL PEPPER AND EGGPLANT RISOTTO)

SERVES 4

The eggplant* is much appreciated all over Italy. But in the north it rarely appears at the table, while in the south it is used in many recipes. When I was researching its botanical origins, I was shocked to discover it is a berry. Imagine. An eggplant is a huge berry. It goes well with tomatoes, potatoes, peppers, and rice. One evening I was invited to Ristorante Stendahl in the village of Collorno, a suburb of Parma. Parma is in Northern Italy. To my surprise, we were served this outrageous risotto. Then the chef came out to meet us. He was born and raised in Messina, Sicily. All at once I understood; Sicilians love eggplant. Wait until you taste this beauty.

1 large red bell pepper

1 large eggplant, unpeeled

1 large scallion, thinly sliced

2 tablespoons olive oil

1½ cups Arborio rice

½ cup dry white wine or
  dry vermouth

1 quart boiling hot chicken stock

Salt and pepper to taste

1 bunch fresh flat leaf parsley

6 leaves fresh basil, chopped

2 tablespoons Pecorino Romano
  cheese, grated

Wash the red pepper. Cut in half, discard seeds and pith. Cut into 1-inch ribbons. Wash the eggplant. Cut into small cubes, place in a colander, sprinkle with 2 tablespoons of salt and leave in sink for ½ hour to leach out its bitter liquid. Melt 1 tablespoon of butter in olive oil in a large saucepan. On moderate heat sauté scallion for five minutes. Add red pepper ribbons and eggplant cubes (after having rinsed them, squeezed them, and dried them with paper towels). Stir and sauté them for eight minutes on high heat. Adjust heat to moderate. Add rice and stir for three minutes. Add wine and cook until it evaporates. Add hot broth, cup by cup, until rice absorbs all of the liquid (about eighteen minutes). Season with salt and

---

*Eggplants are either male or female. Males have more seeds and can be identified by an oval spot at their bottom ends. The females are almost seedless and are much less bitter. Look at its bottom. A small brown round spot indentation identifies its sex as female. Choose the female. They are much sweeter.

pepper. Add 1 tablespoon of butter, the chopped parsley and basil, grated cheese, and the cream. Mix well and remove from heat. Cover and let stand for two minutes. Transfer to warmed serving bowl and bring to table. *Fantastico!* (Fantastic!)

RECOMMENDED WINES:

ALBANA DI ROMAGNA, PINOT NOIR/NERO

Risotto alla Moda Dalamata

(DALMATIAN-STYLE RISOTTO)

SERVES 4

Dalmatia in the former Yugoslavia was once an integral territory of the Kingdom of Italy. It lies directly across the Italian peninsula on the Adriatic Sea. Ethnically, the Dalmatian people are Slavic, but their culture and cuisine are heavily influenced by Italy. I sampled this risotto in an Italian restaurant in the fascinating city of Dubrovnik.

3 tablespoons olive oil	Pinch salt
2 tablespoons butter	½ teaspoon coarsely ground black
1 small onion, minced	pepper
4 ounces lean beef, julienned	1 shot plum brandy or cognac
1 sweet Italian sausage, skinned and	15 ounces long-grain rice
crumbled	1½ quarts boiling hot beef stock
4 ounces lean veal, julienned	½ teaspoon dry rosemary, crushed

In a large saucepan, heat one tablespoon butter and oil on moderate heat. Sauté onion five minutes. Add beef and sausage. Stir and sauté for ten minutes. Add veal and cook another fifteen minutes. Season with salt and pepper. Stir and add brandy. Add rice, stir, and cook for three minutes. Add hot broth, cup by cup, stirring constantly, until rice absorbs all of the liquid (about eighteen minutes). Remove from heat. Mix in remaining tablespoon of butter and rosemary. Transfer to serving bowl and bring to table.

RECOMMENDED WINES:

REFOSCO, PRIMITIVO

Risotto con Fave e Bietole

(FAVA BEAN AND BEET RISOTTO)

SERVES 4

I *first tasted this hearty risotto on a cold, foggy day in Brescia (the birthplace of Pope Paul VI) in the region of Lombardy. It was very tasty and helped ward off the chill of the day.*

2 tablespoons olive oil

1 tablespoon butter

1 tablespoon white lard or fatback, minced (may be omitted)

1 large white onion, thinly sliced

1 16-ounce can or jar of small beets packed in water, drained, washed under cold running water, and dried

5 ounces of jarred or canned fava or broad beans, drained and dried

Salt and pepper

1½ cups Arborio rice

½ cup dry white wine or dry vermouth

1 quart boiling hot chicken stock

1 tablespoon grated Parmesan cheese

1 heaping tablespoon of Pecorino Romano cheese

Heat oil, butter, and lard (if using it) in a large saucepan on gentle heat. Sauté onion five minutes. Add the beets, fava beans, season with salt and pepper and stir. Add the rice and stir three minutes. Add wine, adjust heat to high, and cook until wine evaporates (about three to five minutes). Return heat to moderate. Add boiling hot broth, cup by cup, constantly stirring with wooden spoon, until rice absorbs all the liquid (about eighteen minutes). Sprinkle with grated cheese. Mix well and transfer to deep serving bowl. *Mangia, è molto buono!* (Eat, it's very good!)

RECOMMENDED WINES:

BARBERA, BONARDA/NEBBIOLO BLEND

Risotto del Boscaiolo

(WOODMAN'S RISOTTO)

SERVES 4

Boscaiolo *means woodsman, a man who makes his living off the products of the forests of Italy: raw lumber, forest animals, and of course the wild, earthy mushrooms that are gathered from the decaying debris of the forest floors. Whenever an Italian recipe is named* boscaiolo, *you can be sure it is full of succulent mushrooms. This risotto is redolent of wild mushrooms and is mouthwatering to any fungiphile (mushroom lover).*

2 tablespoons butter	Salt and pepper to taste
1 medium onion, minced	1½ cups Arborio rice
1 large peeled clove garlic, minced	½ cup dry white wine or
2 ounces mortadella or boiled ham, julienned	dry vermouth
	1 quart boiling hot beef broth
10 ounces ordinary white mushrooms, sliced	2 tablespoons light cream
	½ cup chopped fresh flat leaf parsley
1 ounce dried porcini mushrooms, soaked in hot water for ½ hour, drained, washed, and chopped	Pinch of marjoram (½ teaspoon)
	2 tablespoons grated Gruyère or Swiss cheese

In a large saucepan, sauté onion and garlic in butter on moderate heat for five minutes. Add mortadella or ham, stir and cook for two minutes. Add sliced white mushrooms. Sauté on high heat for three minutes, lower heat to gentle and add chopped porcini mushrooms. Season with salt and pepper. Stir. Add rice and stir for three minutes. Add wine and cook until it evaporates. Add hot broth, cup by cup, until rice absorbs all the liquid (about eighteen minutes of constant stirring). Add cream, cheese, parsley, and marjoram. Stir vigorously. Remove from heat. Let rest covered for two minutes. Transfer to serving bowl and bring to the table. Italians prefer not to sprinkle with grated cheese.

RECOMMENDED WINES:

CHIANTI CLASSICO, VINO NOBILE DI MONTEPULCIANO

Risotto con Lattuga

(RISOTTO WITH LETTUCE)

SERVES 4

This recipe comes from Fulvia Sessani of Venice, Italy. This is a very rich dish indeed because of the cream and eggs. But once in a while we all need a respite from retreating from animal fat and avoiding cholesterol. Splurge and enjoy!

4 tablespoons butter

1 small onion, peeled and thinly sliced

1 pound Arborio rice

⅔ cup dry white wine or dry vermouth

1 quart simmering stock (chicken or beef)

1 head romaine lettuce, thinly sliced

⅔ cup freshly grated Parmesan cheese

½ cup light cream

2 egg yolks

Melt the butter in a saucepan and add the onion, then sauté until transparent. Add the rice and stir until it gets shiny. On a high heat, add the wine and stir until it evaporates. Next, on moderate heat, add the broth a little at a time, and stir constantly.

After about ten minutes add the lettuce and cook, stirring, for ten minutes more, until most of the liquid is absorbed by the rice. Add the cream and the yolks, whisk in, and serve.

RECOMMENDED WINES:

SOAVE, SAUVIGNON BLANC

Risotto ai Funghi Marinati Nello Spumante

(MUSHROOMS MARINATED IN DRY CHAMPAGNE RISOTTO)

SERVES 4

Now this is an impressive risotto that should be served at New Year's Eve dinner. Let everyone else have their prime ribs au jus and mashed potatoes. You serve something very special and your guests will make a New Year's resolution to make this risotto for the people they love. Of course, you must serve the risotto with glasses of chilled champagne.

1 pound cultivated white mushrooms (crimini, if you're splurging); 2 days before you make this risotto, wipe the mushrooms clean. Slice them not too thinly. Put them in a plastic food container with a tight fitting lid. Cover with champagne 1 inch over the tops of the mushrooms. Snap on the lid and refrigerate for the 2 days.

4 tablespoons olive oil

1 large clove of peeled garlic, whole

1 large jalapeño pepper (split lengthwise, seeded and ribbed— but be sure to use rubber gloves!)

1½ cups Arborio rice

1½ quarts boiling hot beef stock

1 cup chopped fresh flat leaf parsley

1 tablespoon butter

4 heaping tablespoons grated Parmesan cheese

Heat oil in a large saucepan over moderate heat. Drain the mushrooms, reserving the liquid. Sauté garlic and hot pepper until garlic is very brown. Remove garlic and hot pepper. Add drained, marinated mushrooms and cook them on low heat until they are almost dry. Add rice and stir three minutes. Add reserved champagne marinade and reduce it to three quarters of its volume. Add hot broth, cup by cup, until rice almost absorbs all the liquid, stirring constantly—about eighteen minutes. Remove from heat. Stir in parsley and butter. Add grated cheese. Stir well. Transfer to warmed serving bowl and bring to table. Pop the cork off your best champagne. *Salute. Buon appetito!* (To your health and good appetite!)

Risotto Primavera

(SPRINGTIME RISOTTO)

SERVES 4

Obviously this risotto is prepared with tender springtime veggies. It is very nourishing and substantial. I sampled this recipe one Easter season I spent in Italy, and of course had to get the recipe. I'm glad I did. Now I can share it with you.

1 medium onion, coarsely chopped

2 tablespoons olive oil

4 ounces Italian sweet sausage, skinned and crumbled

1 artichoke, peel off outer leaves, pare to the heart, and julienne

7 ounces shelled peas, fresh or frozen (fully thawed)

2 small carrots, peeled and diced small

Salt and pepper to taste

1½ cups Arborio rice

1 quart boiling hot beef stock

1 tablespoon butter

¼ cup chopped fresh flat leaf parsley

3 tablespoons grated Parmesan cheese

In a large saucepan, sauté onion in olive oil on moderate heat for five minutes. Add sausage and cook for five minutes. Add artichoke, peas, carrots, and seasoning. Cook, stirring, for five minutes. Add rice and stir for three minutes. Add the hot beef stock all at one time. Stir for eighteen minutes. Stir in butter, sprinkle with parsley and grated cheese. Cover and let rest for two minutes. Pour into serving bowl and bring to table.

RECOMMENDED WINES:

CIRÒ CLASSICO, MONTEPULCIANO D'ABRUZZO

Risotto con Rognoni

(VEAL KIDNEY RISOTTO)

SERVES 4

Most Americans avoid organ meats such as kidneys, liver, heart, brains, and sweetbreads. Europeans eat them heartily and consider them delicacies. Be brave! Try this dish and you may change your mind. If you're not brave, substitute Italian sausage for the kidneys.

5 ounces veal kidneys, sliced thinly,
  or
5 ounces Italian sweet sausage,
  skinned and crumbled, browned
  well and drained
½ celery rib, minced
1 small onion, minced
1 ounce pancetta or regular bacon
3 tablespoons olive oil
1 small red bell pepper, seeded, pith
  removed, and julienned

Salt and pepper to taste
2 tablespoons butter
1½ cups Arborio rice
½ cup dry white wine
3 tablespoons shelled peas, fresh or
  frozen
1 quart beef stock, very hot
1 small package saffron (Badia brand
  is great and only costs about $2.49)
¼ cup freshly grated Parmesan
  cheese

In a small nonstick skillet, sauté the kidneys on high heat until they release their liquid and are dry. Wash in warm water, and dry them with paper towels (skip the previous step if using sausage). Set aside. In a large saucepan, place celery, onion, pancetta, oil, and red bell pepper. Cook on gentle heat until everything begins to brown (about eight minutes). Stir in the slices of kidney or sausage. Cook for ten minutes, add salt and pepper, and one tablespoon of butter. Add rice and continuously stir for five minutes. Add wine, adjust heat to moderate, and cook until wine evaporates. Add the peas, stir, and begin to add the broth, a cup at a time, until the rice absorbs most of the liquid. After ten minutes of cooking and stirring, add saffron dissolved in two tablespoons of the hot broth. When twenty minutes have elapsed, the risotto will be ready. Add the rest of the butter and grated cheese. Cover and let rest for two minutes. Pour into a deep serving dish and bring to table.

RECOMMENDED WINES:

BARBERA D'ASTI, BARBARESCO

Risotto con Carciofi e Noci

(ARTICHOKE AND NUT RISOTTO)

SERVES 4

In Southern Italy, most families have their main meal at about one o'clock in the afternoon. All the shops and offices close from 1 P.M. to 4 P.M. Mimy (Domenica) La Bozzetta Gio-vanella, my surrogate mamma Marietta's oldest daughter, invited me to dinner one afternoon at 2 P.M. She told me to come early so that she could teach me this risotto. I am grateful that she did, otherwise, I wouldn't have this knockout recipe for you.

2 tablespoons butter

3 tablespoons olive oil

1 small onion, minced

4 canned artichoke hearts packed in
    water, julienned

2 tablespoons marsala (dry) wine

1½ cups Arborio rice

1 quart boiling hot chicken stock

15 shelled walnuts (should weigh
    about 9 ounces)

Salt and pepper to taste

3 heaping tablespoons cream cheese

2 tablespoons grated Parmesan
    cheese

1 tablespoon fresh flat leaf parsley,
    minced

In a large saucepan on low heat, melt one tablespoon of butter in olive oil. Sauté minced onion for five minutes. Add artichokes, cook gently another five minutes. Add marsala wine; adjust heat to high and evaporate wine (about three minutes). Lower heat to moderate. Add rice. Stir three minutes. Add hot broth, cup by cup, un-til each is absorbed by the rice, stir constantly until all the liquid has been absorbed. Chop the nuts coarsely. Season the risotto with salt and pepper and shut off the heat. In a bowl, whip cream cheese, grated cheese, and chopped walnuts. Add the whipped cheese–nut mixture to the risotto. Stir vigorously. Add remaining tablespoon of but-ter. Stir. Cover and let stand two minutes. Transfer to warmed serving bowl and gar-nish with minced parsley. Serve immediately. *Squisito!* (Exquisite!)

RECOMMENDED WINES:

SAUVIGNON BLANC, PINOT NOIR/NERO

Risotto al Radicchio

(RADICCHIO RISOTTO)

SERVES 4

Radicchio is a slightly bitter red lettuce originally grown on farms and gardens surrounding the city of Treviso in the region of Veneto. Now that it is grown in the United States it has become less expensive and more available. It is terrific in a mixed salad and can be coated with olive oil and grilled. Radicchio makes the risotto very pretty and very scrumptious. Yes, radicchio is still expensive, but a little goes a long way.

2 tablespoons olive oil

4 tablespoons butter

1 large scallion, white bulb and green tops, sliced thin

2 heads radicchio, washed, dried, and coarsely chopped

1½ cups Arborio rice

½ cup dry white wine or dry vermouth

1 quart boiling hot chicken stock

Salt and pepper to taste

2 tablespoons light cream

2 tablespoons grated Parmesan cheese

½ cup chopped fresh flat leaf parsley

In a large saucepan, heat oil and 2 tablespoons of butter on gentle heat. Sauté scallion for 5 minutes. Add radicchio and cook for ten minutes. Add rice and stir for three minutes. Add wine and cook until evaporated. Add hot broth, cup by cup, stirring constantly until rice absorbs all the liquid (about eighteen minutes). Season with salt and pepper. Add cream, grated cheese, parsley, and remaining 2 tablespoons butter. Mix well. Remove from heat. Cover and let stand two minutes. Pour into warm serving bowl and bring to table.

RECOMMENDED WINES:

LUGANA DEL VENETO, GRECO DI TUFO

Risotto con Carote e Piselli

(CARROT AND PEAS RISOTTO)

SERVES 4

I *was sure that you have noticed by now that many of these recipes combine peas and rice. I really prefer to buy fresh peas and shell them myself, but the season for fresh peas is very short. Frozen peas are available throughout the year and come very close to tasting like fresh. I never use canned peas. They are too soft and lack the taste and texture of either fresh or frozen peas.*

1 tablespoon butter	1½ cups Arborio rice
2 tablespoons olive oil	½ cup dry white wine or
2 medium carrots, diced small	dry vermouth
1 large peeled clove garlic, minced	Salt and pepper to taste
1 ounce prosciutto or boiled ham	1 quart boiling hot chicken stock
2 bay leaves	1 heaping tablespoon grated
7 ounces frozen peas,	Parmesan cheese
completely thawed	2 tablespoons light cream or
2 canned, peeled Italian plum	half-and-half
tomatoes, chopped	

Melt butter in oil in large saucepan on gentle heat. Adjust heat to moderate and add carrots, celery, garlic, onion, and prosciutto. Sauté for eight minutes. Add bay leaves and peas. Cook for one minute. Add tomatoes. Cook for five minutes. Add rice and stir three minutes. Add wine and cook until it evaporates (about five minutes). Season with salt and pepper. Add hot stock, cup by cup, constantly stirring with wooden spoon, until rice absorbs almost all the liquid (about eighteen minutes). Remove bay leaves. Sprinkle with grated cheese. Stir. Add the cream. Stir vigorously. Transfer to a deep serving bowl and bring to table. You may provide grated Parmesan for those who desire it.

RECOMMENDED WINES:

SANGIOVESE DI ROMAGNA, DOLCETTO D'ALBA

Risotto del Convento

(MONASTERY RISOTTO)

SERVES 4

In Frosinone, a town in the region of Campania, I was invited to visit the Monastery of Casamari. It was built on the summit of a mountain overlooking the town over seven hundred years ago. It belongs to the Cistercian order of monks and is self-sufficient. The white and black habited monks raise all their own food and run a huge distillery that produces unparalleled liqueurs sold to the public. I was the guest of the abbot-general and was given the rooms that the Pope uses when he visits. I was impressed at being welcomed like a brother. I was even more impressed that evening when I tasted this risotto.

1 tablespoon butter

2 tablespoons olive oil

7 ounces small fresh beets, peeled
and julienned

1 yellow bell pepper, seeded, pith
removed, halved, and julienned

1 leek, white bulb only, quartered,
washed well, dried and thinly
sliced

1 heart of romaine lettuce, washed,
dried, and julienned

Salt and pepper to taste

1½ cups Arborio rice

½ cup dry white wine or
dry vermouth

1 quart boiling hot chicken stock

1 tablespoon grated Swiss cheese

2 paper-thin slices Swiss cheese,
julienned

Melt butter in oil in a large saucepan on gentle heat. Sauté beets, bell pepper, leek, lettuce, for 8 minutes. Season with salt and pepper. Add rice and stir 3 minutes. Add wine, adjust heat to high and cook until wine evaporates. Adjust heat to moderate. Add hot stock, cup by cup, stirring constantly until rice absorbs all the liquid (about eighteen minutes). Remove from heat. Stir in grated and julienned cheese. Stir vigorously. Cover and let rest two minutes. Transfer to serving bowl and bring to table. *Benedetto!* (Blessed!)

RECOMMENDED WINES:

MERLOT, CANNONAOU DI SARDEGNA

Risotto con Piselli e Carciofi

(PEAS AND ARTICHOKE RISOTTO)

SERVES 4

For this recipe I use frozen artichoke hearts because they most resemble the fresh. I tasted this risotto at a restaurant named Alla Vedova ("at the widow's") in Udine, the capital of the region of Friuli Venezia Giulia. The widow was there, boy was she there! She ran the whole place by herself. She cooked, served, and cleaned up. She was not a "merry widow" until I talked to her in my Calabrian-accented Italian. She broke out in a broad, genuine smile and spoke to me in the Calabrian dialect. She was born and raised in Pellaro di Reggio Calabria only one mile south of my mom and pop's hometown. She sat down and ate with me and shared a bottle of Cirò (the classic wine from Calabria). I made a friend who insisted that no paisano could pay the bill. It was on her. Thank you, Filomena Laganà.

1 tablespoon butter	1 chicken bouillon cube, crumbled
2 tablespoons olive oil	Salt and pepper to taste
2 small white onions, thinly sliced	½ cup chopped flat leaf parsley
1 large clove garlic, thinly sliced	1½ cups Arborio rice
7 ounces frozen peas, completely thawed	½ cup dry white wine
	1 quart boiling hot chicken stock
4 frozen artichoke hearts, completely thawed and julienned	½ pound mozzarella cheese, cubed
	¼ cup chopped fresh mint leaves

In a large saucepan, melt butter in oil on gentle heat. Sauté onions and garlic for five minutes. Add peas and artichokes. Stir and cook for five minutes. Sprinkle crumbled bouillon cube on the mixture. Season with salt and pepper. Sprinkle with chopped parsley. Add rice and stir three minutes. Adjust heat to high. Add wine and cook until it evaporates (three minutes). Adjust heat to low. Add hot broth, cup by cup, constantly stirring until all the broth is absorbed (about eighteen minutes). Remove from heat. Stir in mozzarella cheese and mint. Cover and let rest two minutes. Transfer to serving bowl and bring to table.

RECOMMENDED WINES:

BIANCO DI GIALLA (FRIULI), REISLING ITALICO

Risotto con Melanzane e Prezzemolo

(EGGPLANT AND PARSLEY RISOTTO)

SERVES 4

Eggplant is a marvelous, tangy meat substitute for the vegetarian or non-vegetarian. We're not going to get into a religious argument here. Some vegetarians, or vegans (stricter fundamentalists who avoid any animal products such as eggs or dairy), are as fanatical about their beliefs as some Christians, Jews, and Moslems are about theirs. This tasty risotto is for everyone, regardless of belief systems. Please don't get so serious. It will bother your digestion.

1 tablespoon butter	½ cup dry white wine
2 tablespoons olive oil	1 quart boiling hot chicken stock
1 small onion, chopped	1 cup fresh flat leaf parsley, chopped
2 large cloves garlic, crushed	Pinch of oregano
2 medium eggplants, peeled and diced small	2 heaping tablespoons freshly grated Parmesan cheese
1½ cups Arborio rice	Salt and pepper to taste

In a large saucepan, melt butter in oil on gentle heat. Sauté onion and garlic eight minutes. Add eggplant cubes, stir, and cook for eight more minutes. Add rice and stir three minutes. Add wine, adjust heat to high, and cook until wine evaporates. Adjust heat to low and add hot stock, cup by cup, until rice absorbs all the liquid (about eighteen minutes of constant stirring). Near the end of this cooking time, add parsley, oregano, and grated cheese. Season with salt and pepper. Stir vigorously and transfer to a deep serving bowl. Bring to table.

RECOMMENDED WINES:

PINOT GRIGIO, CHARDONNAY

Risotto con Verdure Miste

(MIXED GREENS RISOTTO)

SERVES 4

This is one of my favorite risotti because I love vegetables. Over the years, after living in rectories (homes for unwed Fathers), this Father got bored with meat and potatoes for supper almost every night. Sometimes the cook would serve potatoes and meat just for a change. I now try to avoid red meats, not because the American Heart Association suggests it, but because I've lost my taste for it.

2 tablespoons olive oil

2 tablespoons butter

1 small onion, chopped

2 scallions, thinly sliced

1 bunch *broccoli di rape* (broccoli rabe), washed thoroughly and chopped

2 zucchini, skin on and diced

½ green bell pepper, seeded, pithed, and diced

1 medium carrot, peeled and diced

2 ribs celery, diced

3 tablespoons frozen peas, thawed

1½ cups Arborio rice

Salt and pepper to taste

3 cups boiling hot chicken stock

½ cup chopped fresh flat leaf parsley

½ cup chopped fresh basil leaves

In a large saucepan, melt one tablespoon of butter in oil on gentle heat. Sauté onion, scallions, broccoli rabe, zucchini, bell pepper, carrot, celery, and peas for eight minutes. Add rice and season with salt and pepper. Stir for five minutes. Add all the stock. Adjust heat to low. Simmer covered for twenty minutes. Remove from heat. Stir in parsley and basil. Add remaining tablespoon of butter. Stir vigorously. Transfer to serving bowl and bring to table. Yes, your guests can sprinkle grated Parmesan or Pecorino Romano cheese, but only if you put it on the table.

RECOMMENDED WINES:

VERMENTINO, GAVI DI GAVI

Risotto alla Moda Turchese

(TURKISH-STYLE RISOTTO)

SERVES 4

Brindisi is the largest port city on the Adriatic Sea. From there ships sail to Greece and Turkey. This is an interesting and tasty Italian risotto named "Turkish-Style" because Turkish tourists visiting Brindisi seem to love this risotto. Even though their Muslim dietary laws rule out pork, they disobey the law of the Koran and know they will repent and be forgiven.

3 ounces Italian hot sausage

1 large peeled onion

1 large peeled clove garlic

2 tablespoons butter

2 tablespoons olive oil

10 ounces cultivated white mushrooms

1 small eggplant, unpeeled, washed, and diced small

½ yellow bell pepper, seeded, pith removed, washed, and diced small

1 bay leaf

1 quart boiling hot beef stock

4 Italian plum tomatoes, canned and chopped

Pinch of salt and pepper

1½ cups Arborio rice

1 shot glass good gin (Bombay is best, I think)

2 heaping tablespoons grated Parmesan cheese

1 tablespoon chopped fresh flat leaf parsley

Skin the sausage and mince the meat. Heat one tablespoon of butter and oil in a large saucepan and add the onion and garlic that have been minced together. Sauté for five minutes on gentle heat. Add sausage and cook eight minutes. Add the cultivated mushrooms, which were wiped with paper towel and chopped, the eggplant and yellow pepper previously small diced. Add bay leaf. Stir with wooden spoon and brown for ten minutes on moderate heat. Add a few tablespoons of hot broth occasionally. Discard bay leaf. Add chopped tomatoes. Season with salt and pepper. Stir for three minutes. Add rice, stir another three minutes. Add gin and cook on high heat for four minutes. Add hot broth, cup by cup, stirring constantly for eighteen minutes, until rice absorbs all the liquid. Add grated cheese and remaining tablespoon of butter. Stir well. Cover, remove from heat, and let rest for two minutes. Transfer to warmed serving bowl. Garnish with parsley and bring to table. You don't have to be Turkish to enjoy this risotto. You may sprinkle more grated cheese if you wish.

RECOMMENDED WINES:

SALICE SALENTINO RISERVA, AGLIANICO DEL VULTURE (BASILICATA)

Risotto al Sapore di Tonno

(TUNA-FLAVORED RISOTTO)

SERVES 4

Do *you like tuna? I like tuna, but I can't abide tuna casseroles. This is not a tuna casserole. It's a magnificent and easy way to prepare a risotto. The tuna happily gives up its flesh to flavor this dish. Thank you, Charlie Tuna!*

1 garlic clove

1 bunch fresh flat leaf parsley, washed well

3 tablespoons olive oil

1 6-ounce can tuna packed in oil, drained and flaked

3½ cups Arborio rice

1 quart boiling hot beef stock

1 tablespoon butter

Salt and pepper to taste

Mince the garlic and parsley leaves together or place in the bowl of a food processor fitted with steel blade and pulse for one minute. Heat olive oil in skillet on moderate heat. Add garlic and parsley and sauté gently for five minutes. Add flaked tuna and rice. Stir for five minutes to coat rice evenly with oil. Transfer to a large saucepan and on moderate heat, begin to add boiling stock, cup by cup, stirring constantly until all stock is absorbed (about eighteen minutes). Add butter, salt and pepper to taste, stir, cover and let rest two minutes. Transfer to serving bowl and bring to table. No grated cheese, please.

RECOMMENDED WINES:

BIANCO DI SICILIA (INZOLIA/CATARRATTO BLEND), FIANO DI AVELLINO

Risotto Alla Bella Elena

(BEAUTIFUL HELEN'S RISOTTO)

SERVES 4

*H*elen of Troy was so beautiful that her face launched a thousand ships in the war between ancient Greece and Troy. This risotto named for her won't start a war—well maybe only a little squabble at your table over who is going to get a second serving.

2 tablespoons olive oil

1 tablespoon butter

1 medium red bell pepper, seeded, cut in half, pith removed, and diced small

1 large peeled white onion, thinly sliced

1 large peeled clove garlic, crushed

2 heaping tablespoons frozen peas, completely thawed

1 rib celery, diced small

½ cup chopped fresh flat leaf parsley

½ cup chopped fresh basil leaves

1½ cups Arborio rice

½ cup dry white wine

1 quart boiling hot chicken stock

Salt and pepper to taste

2 small packages saffron, dissolved in 2 tablespoons hot broth (Badia brand, 0.008 gram per package)

2 tablespoons light cream

4 heaping tablespoons grated Parmesan cheese

Heat oil and butter in a large saucepan on gentle heat. Sauté red bell pepper, onion, garlic, peas, celery, parsley, and basil on moderate heat for eight minutes. Lower heat to simmer. Stir in rice and mix three minutes. Add wine and cook until wine evaporates (about five minutes). Add hot broth, cup by cup, constantly stirring with wooden spoon, until rice absorbs all the liquid (about eighteen minutes). Season with salt and pepper. Stir in saffron dissolved in two tablespoons of hot broth. Stir in cream and grated cheese. Cover and allow to rest for two minutes. Transfer to a deep serving dish and bring to table. Oh, Helen! Oh, Helen!

RECOMMENDED WINES:

RIESLING, PINOT BIANCO

Risotto ai Finocchi
(FENNEL RISOTTO)

SERVES 4

I *was on my way to spend a few days in Siracusa, on the southern coast of Sicily. I was about halfway there, somewhere between Taormina and Siracusa. It was November and the temperature was about seventy. I kept passing trucks loaded with fresh fennel; the aroma of that sweet herb filled the air, overcoming the fumes of diesel and gasoline and making me impatient for dinner. After arriving in Siracusa and getting settled in the hotel, my first move was to get to the kind of family-run restaurant the Italians call a trattoria and order this risotto. It was delectable then; it's delectable when I make it at home now.*

2 tablespoons butter	Salt and pepper to taste
2 tablespoons olive oil	½ cup warm beer
2 tablespoons pancetta or bacon, finely minced	1 quart boiling hot chicken stock
2 small fresh fennel bulbs, trimmed, boiled for 10 minutes in lightly salted water, dried, and julienned	3 tablespoons grated Gruyére or Swiss cheese
	Pinch of fennel seeds (⅛ teaspoon)
1½ cups Arborio rice	2 tablespoons light cream

In a large saucepan, melt one tablespoon of butter in oil on gentle heat. Sauté pancetta for five minutes. Add julienned fennel and sauté for ten minutes. Add rice and stir three minutes. Season with salt and pepper. Add beer, adjust heat to high and cook until beer evaporates. Adjust heat to low. Add hot stock, cup by cup, until rice absorbs all the liquid (about eighteen minutes constantly stirring). Remove from heat. Add grated cheese, fennel seeds, cream, and remaining tablespoon of butter. Stir vigorously. Cover and allow to set for two minutes. Transfer to deep serving bowl and bring to table. *Delicato, rinfrescante!* (Delicate and refreshing!) Yes, you may sprinkle with grated Parmesan cheese.

RECOMMENDED WINES:

BIANCO DI SICILIA (INZOLIA/CATARRATTO BLEND), TOCAI

Risotto del Goloso

(THE GLUTTON'S RISOTTO)

SERVES 4

A *real glutton would eat this whole delectable risotto all by himself. The sin of gluttony is defined as eating until the point of getting sick. Now, remember, I am a priest and I don't want you to commit any sins, but virture isn't virtue unless it is tested. This risotto will be a real test of your virtue of self-control. Okay. End of sermon. Let's eat!*

1 tablespoon butter

2 tablespoons olive oil

1 large peeled onion, thinly sliced

1 large peeled clove garlic, crushed

1 tablespoon pancetta or bacon, minced

4 small carrots, peeled and diced small

Pinch of salt (⅛ teaspoon)

1½ cups Arborio rice

½ cup dry white wine or dry vermouth

1 quart boiling hot chicken stock

2 tablespoons heavy cream

2 tablespoons grated Parmesan cheese

1 tablespoon chopped fresh chervil or flat leaf parsley

In a large saucepan, melt butter in oil on gentle heat. Sauté onion, garlic, and pancetta for eight minutes. Add carrots and pinch of salt and cook for ten minutes. Add a few tablespoons of your hot broth if it gets too dry. Add wine. Add rice and stir three minutes. Add hot broth, cup by cup, stirring constantly, until rice absorbs all the liquid (about eighteen minutes). Remove from heat, stir in cream, cheese, and chervil. Stir well. Transfer to serving bowl and bring to table. Remember now, a little self-control! No need for extra grated cheese.

RECOMMENDED WINES:

BARBERA D'ALBA, VALPOLICELLA

Risotto del Buongustaio

(GOURMET'S RISOTTO)

SERVES 4

I *do not consider myself a gourmet, although a reviewer of my book* Father Orsini's Italian Kitchen *(New York: St. Martin's Press, 1993) said, "Father Orsini reminds me of the gourmet priest who sends the wine back at Mass." All kidding aside, this is a gourmet's delight.*

5 ounces boiled ham (I like Krakus brand Polish ham), julienned	Pepper to taste
2 tablespoons butter	½ cup light cream
2 tablespoons olive oil	1 tablespoon butter to finish
1 medium white onion, thinly sliced	2 tablespoons grated Parmesan cheese
1¾ cups Arborio rice	2 tablespoons grated Gruyère or Swiss cheese
1 quart boiling hot beef stock	

In a large saucepan, sauté the ham in butter and oil for five minutes. Remove the ham with a slotted spoon and set aside. Sauté the onion on gentle heat for eight minutes. Add rice and, stirring, let the grains be coated with the fat for five minutes. Add the boiling hot beef stock cup by cup, stirring constantly, until the rice absorbs all the liquid, about eighteen minutes. Add pepper to taste. Add cream. Stir and cook another three minutes. Remove from heat. Add cooked ham strips. Stir. Add butter and the two cheeses. Stir well. Pour into a serving bowl and bring to table. No extra cheese!

RECOMMENDED WINES:

BARBERA D'ASTI, BAROLO

Risotto al Diavolicchio

(DEVILED RISOTTO)

SERVES 4

We travel back to Southern Italy, namely the unforgettable peninsula of Sorrento in the province of Naples, for this deviled (meaning burning, spicy, hot) risotto. If you are enamored of spicy, hot dishes, this one's for you, but save some for me.

2 tablespoons olive oil

1 tablespoon butter

1 medium peeled onion, chopped

1 large jalapeño pepper, minced,
    seeds and all

1½ cups Arborio rice

½ cup dry white wine or
    dry vermouth

3 ounces hot sopresatta (salami),
    minced

5 ounces pitted black olives,
    cut into rings

1 quart boiling hot beef stock

Salt and pepper to taste

2 tablespoons light cream

½ cup chopped flat leaf parsley

4 heaping tablespoons grated
    Pecorino Romano cheese

Place a 6-quart saucepan on gentle heat and melt butter in olive oil. Add onion and hot pepper. Sauté for five minutes. Add rice, stir for three minutes. Add wine and cook until it evaporates. Add hot salami and olives. Cook another five minutes. Now add hot broth, cup by cup, stirring constantly for eighteen minutes until the rice has absorbed all the liquid. Season with salt and pepper. One minute before turning off the heat, add cream and parsley. Stir in well. Remove from heat. Sprinkle with grated cheese and serve immediately. *Piccante!* (Hot stuff!)

RECOMMENDED WINES:

TAURASI, CIRÓ RISERVA

Risotto con Piselli e Spinaci
(PEAS AND SPINACH RISOTTO)

SERVES 4

Pisa, in the region of Tuscany, is most famous for its Leaning Tower. When I was there, I noticed that everything leans: the cathedral, the baptistery, and the city hall. (Even the citizens, I noticed, lean . . . only kidding about the people!) I sampled this delicious Pisan risotto in a small out-of-the-way family restaurant (trattoria) and when I walked out I was leaning! It was probably the two glasses of homemade white wine that the owner brought to my table and didn't charge me for.

1 tablespoon butter	Salt and pepper to taste
2 tablespoons olive oil	1½ cups Arborio rice
1 carrot, peeled and minced	½ cup dry white wine or dry
1 rib celery, minced	vermouth
1 medium onion, peeled and minced	1 quart boiling hot chicken stock
1 clove peeled garlic, minced	2 tablespoons grated Parmesan
3 ounces frozen spinach, thawed and	cheese
minced	2 tablespoons light cream
3 ounces frozen peas, thawed	

Sauté minced carrots, celery, onion, spinach, and garlic in butter and oil in a large saucepan on moderate heat for eight minutes. Add peas. Season with salt and pepper. Add rice, stir for three minutes. Add wine, cook until evaporated. Add hot broth, cup by cup, stirring constantly until rice absorbs all the liquid (about eighteen minutes). Stir in cheese and cream. Transfer to serving bowl and bring to table. No extra grated cheese, unless you insist!

RECOMMENDED WINES:

CHARDONNAY, GRECCHETTO

Risotto di Bolzano
(BOLZANO RISOTTO)

SERVES 4

If the ingredients for this risotto speak with an Austrian accent, remember it comes from Bolzano. Bolzano is the capital of the region of Trento-Alto Adrige which was part of the Austro–Hungarian Empire for centuries. The local language is German. Even the street signs are bilingual (Italian and German). This risotto should be accompanied by a glass of beer while you are listening to a German oompah band.

½ white peeled onion, thinly sliced

2 tablespoons butter

2 tablespoons olive oil (this is still Italy)

6 Vienna sausages in thin slices (I prefer Goya brand)

1½ cups Arborio rice

1 cup of beer (warm)

1 quart boiling hot beef stock

3 ounces grated Swiss cheese (Emmentaler)

Salt and pepper to taste

In a large saucepan, sauté onion gently in 1 tablespoon butter and oil for five minutes. Add Vienna sausages and cook for five minutes. Add rice and stir for five minutes to coat rice with oil. Add the beer. Adjust heat to moderate and cook until beer evaporates. Add boiling hot beef stock, cup by cup, continuously stirring until all stock is absorbed, about eighteen minutes. It will be a little liquidy. Add cheese, remaining butter, salt, and pepper to taste. Stir vigorously. Pour into serving bowl and serve. *Wunderbar!* (Wonderful!)

RECOMMENDED WINES:

TRAMINER, GEWÜRZTRAMINER

Risotto al Barolo

(BAROLO WINE RISOTTO)

SERVES 4

This is very serious cooking with wine. In fact you have to use half a bottle of wine; the other half is the cook's privilege to sip while he or she does all the stirring required. This is a unique risotto both in color and in taste.

½ peeled onion, minced	4 tablespoons grated Parmesan
1½ cups Arborio rice	cheese
½ a 750-ml. bottle of Barolo red wine	Salt and pepper to taste
½ quart boiling hot beef stock	

Sauté the onion in a large saucepan in two tablespoons butter on gentle heat for five minutes. Add rice and stir to coat the grains with butter. Adjust heat to moderate and begin to add the wine ¼ cup at a time, continuously stirring, until all the wine is used and has evaporated. Add the hot broth in the same manner until it is all used and the rice has absorbed it. This will take about eighteen minutes. Add one tablespoon butter, grated cheese, and salt and pepper to taste. Pour into serving bowl and bring to table. *Fantastico!* (Fantastic!)

RECOMMENDED WINE:

BAROLO

Risotto del Reverendo ✤

(THE REVEREND'S RISOTTO)

SERVES 4

When I stay in Reggio Calabria, I reside in the Casa del Clero (the clergy house). It is the residence of the retired bishop and home to elderly retired priests. But Monsignor Giuseppe Caruso, my dear friend, always allows me to stay there at a minimum cost. One afternoon, Sister Lucia, the nun in charge of the residence, called me on the intercom to come to the kitchen because the retired bishop, the Most Reverend Sorrentino, was cooking the main course. I never watched a bishop cook, so I rushed to the kitchen. There was the bishop dressed in his purple cassock and skull cap, a huge apron wrapped around his ample paunch.

1 tablespoon minced pancetta or bacon	½ cup dry white wine
1 tablespoon butter	1 quart boiling hot chicken stock
2 tablespoons olive oil	1 can pinto beans, drained (15 ounces)
1 rib celery, minced	3 tablespoons grated Pecorino Romano cheese
5 ounces savoy cabbage, sliced into ribbons	Pinch of salt
1 small onion, minced	1 tablespoon coarse ground black pepper
1½ cups Arborio rice	

In a large saucepan, sauté pancetta, celery, cabbage, and onion in butter and oil for eight minutes on moderate heat. Stir in rice for three minutes. Add wine and cook until it evaporates. Add hot broth, cup by cup, until rice absorbs all the liquid. After nine minutes of constant stirring, add drained beans. When rice is done after nine more minutes of stirring, add grated cheese and stir vigorously. Season with salt and pepper. Remove from heat, say a short prayer (the bishop did), turn into serving bowl, and serve. *Benedetto risotto!* (A blessed risotto!)

RECOMMENDED WINES:

GRECO DI TUFO, FIANO DI AVELLINO

Risotto con Funghi, Prosciutto, e Mozzarella
(MUSHROOM, PROSCIUTTO, AND MOZZARELLA RISOTTO)

SERVES 4

L'Aquila, a jewel of a town in the Abruzzi region, is not on the usual Italy tour track. Here lies the incorrupt remains of Saint Bernardine of Siena, who was a great Franciscan preacher and the founder of the Catholic World-Wide Holy Name Society. I visited a rustic and charming Abruzzese *restaurant in Montereale (a suburb in the mountains of L'Aquila). The family who ran the restaurant exemplified the gracious sincerity and simplicity of those who dwell in the isolation of mountain villages. This risotto was the rich main course.*

10 ounces regular white mushrooms	1 quart boiling hot chicken stock
1 garlic clove, peeled	3½ ounces prosciutto or boiled ham
1 small onion, peeled	cut into julienne strips
2 tablespoons olive oil	1 pound mozzarella cheese, cut into
1 tablespoon butter	small cubes
1 ounce dried porcini mushrooms	2 tablespoons light cream
Pinch of salt	2 tablespoons grated Parmesan
1½ cups Arborio rice	cheese
½ cup dry white wine	½ cup chopped flat leaf parsley

Wipe the mushrooms with a paper towel and slice from top to bottom, including the stems. Chop the garlic and onion, then sauté in oil and butter in a large saucepan on gentle heat for five minutes. Add the cultivated mushrooms, sauté on high heat for two minutes. Add dried mushrooms (previously soaked in warm water for half an hour, drained, washed, and chopped). Add pinch of salt and stir. Add rice and stir for three minutes. Add wine and cook until it evaporates. Add hot broth, cup by cup, constantly stirring until rice absorbs all the liquid (about eighteen minutes). During the last three minutes of cooking, add julienned ham and the mozzarella cut into small cubes, the cream, and the grated cheese. Mix well. Transfer to serving bowl, garnish with chopped parsley. Serve immediately. This is an authentic taste of the Abruzzi mountains.

RECOMMENDED WINES:

CHIANTI RISERVA, PREDICATO DI BITURICA (CABERNET/SANGIOVESE BLEND)

Risotto Brindisano

(RISOTTO FROM BRINDISI)

SERVES 4

Brindisi is a major port city in the region of Apulia. Ships leaving the port travel all over the world. I was invited to board a ship that had just returned from India and dine with the captain. The ship's cook brought us this Italian risotto with a touch of Indian flavor.

1 small onion, minced	Salt and pepper to taste
1 large clove garlic, minced	1 quart boiling hot chicken stock
1 rib celery, minced	1 level teaspoon curry powder
1 tablespoon butter	dissolved in ½ cup hot broth
2 tablespoons olive oil	(beef or chicken)
1½ cups Arborio rice	½ cup fresh flat leaf parsley, finely
½ cup dry white wine	chopped
4 ripe Italian tomatoes, peeled	
(or canned)	

In a large saucepan, sauté onion, garlic, and celery in butter and oil on moderate heat for eight minutes. Add rice and stir for three minutes. Add hot broth, cup by cup, constantly stirring for eighteen minutes. After nine minutes, add dissolved curry. When finished cooking and rice is al dente, add parsley and stir vigorously. Pour into serving bowl, bring to table and dig in. *Buono abbastanza!* (Good enough!)

RECOMMENDED WINES:

SALICE SALENTINO, PRIMITIVO

Risotto ai Peperoni

(RED BELL PEPPER RISOTTO)

SERVES 4

This dish has spectacular eye appeal and tantalizes the tastebuds. I tasted it when I was invited to accompany Sandro La Bozzetta and his wife, Clelia, to supper at the home of their Neapolitan friends living in Reggio Calabria. A friendly argument broke out about the origin of the risotto. Naples, Venice, and Reggio Calabria were the contenders. I voted for Venice and got booed. Make this risotto and you'll get applause.

1 large onion, minced

2 tablespoons butter

2 tablespoons olive oil

2 medium red bell peppers, halved, pith removed, seeded, and julienned

Salt and pepper to taste

1½ cups Arborio rice

½ cup dry white wine

1 quart boiling hot beef stock

1 tablespoon pitted black olives, chopped

Pinch marjoram or oregano

2 tablespoons light cream

3 tablespoons grated Parmesan cheese

In a large saucepan, sauté the onion in butter and olive oil for five minutes. Add the red bell peppers and cook on moderate heat for fifteen minutes. Season with salt and pepper. Add the rice and stir to coat each grain with fat. Add wine and cook until it evaporates. Add the hot stock, cup by cup, stirring continuously until all the broth has been absorbed (about eighteen minutes). Add the olives, marjoram, and cream and mix thoroughly. Sprinkle with grated cheese, stir, and cover. Let rest two minutes before serving.

RECOMMENDED WINES:

VALPOLICELLA, CIRÓ CLASSICO

Risotto in Campo Verde

(RISOTTO IN A GREEN FIELD)

SERVES 4

This imaginative name comes from the green color of the peas, parsley, and basil. It's a pretty name and a delectable risotto. Green is the color that signifies hope and the beginning of new life in the spring. Well this dish will have you hoping for more and put a spring to your step.

3 tablespoons butter

1 medium onion, thinly sliced

1½ cups Arborio rice

1 quart boiling hot beef stock

1 pound shelled frozen peas, thawed
   completely

½ cup fresh flat leaf parsley, chopped

¾ cup fresh basil leaves, chopped

3 tablespoons grated Parmesan
   cheese.

Sauté the onion in two tablespoons of butter in a large saucepan on low heat. Add rice and stir for three minutes. Add the hot stock, cup by cup, stirring continuously for eighteen minutes or until all liquid is absorbed. Add parsley, basil, and grated cheese. Mix well. Cover and let rest for two minutes. Pour into serving bowl and bring to table.

RECOMMENDED WINES:

LUGANA DEL VENETO, SOAVE

Risotto ai Tre Formaggi

(THREE-CHEESE RISOTTO)

SERVES 4

A *recent* New York Times *article reported that scientists made a study in France where huge amounts of cheese are consumed, and to their surprise they found that the French suffer less coronary disease than most Europeans, except Southern Italians. It seems that the bacteria and enzymes in cheese render the cholesterol in fresh whole milk harmless. They also said that the daily consumption of red wine may be an additional important factor in preventing heart disease. I think that's great news for cheese and red-wine lovers. It made me very happy. I was even happier when I had it for dinner.*

2 tablespoons olive oil	Salt and pepper to taste
1 tablespoon butter	1 heaping tablespoon mascarpone or
1 small onion, thinly sliced	cream cheese
1 large clove garlic, crushed	2 heaping tablespoons Gorgonzola or
1½ cups Arborio rice	other blue cheese
½ cup dry white wine	1 heaping tablespoon freshly grated
1 quart boiling hot chicken stock	Parmesan cheese

In a large saucepan, melt butter in oil on gentle heat. Sauté onion and garlic for five minutes. Add rice and stir three minutes. Add wine, adjust heat to moderate, and cook until it evaporates. Add hot stock, cup by cup, constantly stirring, until rice absorbs all the liquid (about eighteen minutes). Season with salt and pepper. Remove from heat. Add the three cheeses. Mix vigorously. Transfer to serving bowl and bring to table. Eat to your heart's content.

RECOMMENDED WINES:

AMARONE, BAROLO

Risotto al Cumino

(FRESH CUMIN RISOTTO)

SERVES 4

Cumin is a small, grassy plant that produces seeds that are used in making the liqueur kümmel and much used in Latin-American cooking. This risotto absolutely requires fresh cumin, which grows abundantly in spring on the plateau of Asiago. If you can't get fresh cumin, just skip this recipe. There are no satisfactory substitutes.

1 medium onion, thinly sliced	1½ cups Arborio rice
3 tablespoons butter	1 quart boiling hot beef stock
3 tablespoons olive oil	Pinch of salt
1 cup chopped fresh cumin	2 tablespoons grated Asiago cheese
1 cup dry white wine	

Sauté onion in 1½ tablespoons of butter and the oil in a large saucepan on gentle heat for five minutes. Add chopped cumin, stir, and sauté three minutes. Add wine and cook for five minutes. Add rice, stir to coat the grains with fat. Over moderate heat, add hot broth, cup by cup, stirring constantly, until all the broth is totally absorbed by the rice. (This should take eighteen minutes from the first cup of stock to the last.) Add pinch of salt. Add the remaining 1½ tablespoons of butter and grated cheese. Give a last stir and bring immediately to the table.

RECOMMENDED WINES:

BARBARESCO, GATTINARA

Risotto con Funghi alla Mia Maniera

(MUSHROOM RISOTTO MY WAY)

SERVES 4

Frank Sinatra made the song "My Way" one of the most successful popular songs in modern musical history. Although it was written by Paul Anka, "My Way" was and is always associated with "Old Blue Eyes." Whoever invented this recipe, did it "their way." I am sure you will claim it for yourself.

1 cup dried porcini mushrooms reconstituted in a cup of warm water for ½ hour. Drain, pour the soaking liquid through a fine wire mesh sieve lined with two layers of paper towels, and reserve the liquid.

3 tablespoons butter

1 tablespoon olive oil

Salt and pepper to taste

½ cup chopped fresh flat leaf parsley

1 small clove garlic, minced

1 small onion, minced

1½ cups Arborio rice

½ cup dry white wine

1 quart boiling hot beef stock

3 tablespoons grated Parmesan cheese

Wash the mushrooms under cold running water. Chop mushrooms and sauté in one tablespoon of butter and olive oil in small skillet on moderate heat for five minutes. Season with salt and pepper. Add parsley and garlic. Cook five more minutes. Set aside. In a large saucepan, sauté onion in one tablespoon of butter on gentle heat for five minutes. Add rice and stir for three minutes. Add wine and cook until it evaporates. Add reserved mushroom liquid and cook until it evaporates. Begin adding hot beef stock, cup by cup, until all the broth is absorbed by the rice (about eighteen minutes), constantly stirring. During the last five minutes, add the contents of the skillet which was used to sauté mushrooms. Add remaining tablespoon of butter and grated Parmesan cheese. Stir, then allow to rest two minutes covered. Pour into a preheated serving bowl and bring to table.

RECOMMENDED WINES:

BARBERA D'ASTI, DOLCETTO D'ALBA

Risotto al Forno di Clelia

(CLELIA'S BAKED RISOTTO)

SERVES 6

I *traveled to Italy in January 1993 to visit my relatives in Reggio Calabria. On Monday, January 18, I was invited to dinner at my* compare *Sandro's house. I watched as his wife, Clelia, prepared this stupendous baked risotto. When I tasted it, I thought,* It doesn't get any better than this. I am surrounded by people who love me and I am eating the best food in the world. Thank you, God. I am truly blessed. *Now I share this blessing with you; share it in turn with people you love.*

1 large peeled onion, sliced thinly	4 tablespoons butter
3 tablespoons olive oil	3 slices boiled ham, julienned
1½ cups Arborio rice	5 slices domestic provolone cheese or
1 cup dry white wine	Swiss, julienned
1 quart boiling hot stock	½ pound mozzarella cheese, diced
(chicken or beef)	4 tablespoons Pecorino Romano
½ cup milk	cheese
1 small package saffron (Badia	
brand, 0.0008 gram)	

Preheat oven to 350°. In a large saucepan, sauté onion in olive oil on moderate heat for five minutes. Add rice and stir for three minutes. Add wine and cook until it evaporates. Add boiling stock, cup by cup, until rice absorbs all the stock, stirring constantly. This takes about eighteen minutes of constant stirring. Add half the milk with the last cup of broth. Remove from heat, add saffron and mix well. Set aside. Butter a baking dish with one tablespoon of butter. Make a layer of rice on bottom of dish, dot with remaining butter, place the ham and the provolone or Swiss cheese on rice, distributed evenly. Cover with diced mozzarella cheese, pour remaining milk over the surface. Cover with the rest of the rice. Sprinkle with grated Pecorino Romano cheese. Bake for forty minutes. Remove and let rest for ten minutes, cut, and serve. *Magnifico!* (Magnificent!)

RECOMMENDED WINES:

MONTEPULCIANO, CHIANTI CLASSICO

Risotto della Tata ✿

(THE NANNY'S RISOTTO)

SERVES 4

The upper middle class in Italy often hire a nanny (whose job it is to cook, clean, and help raise the children). Marietta La Bozzetta's oldest daughter, Mimy, has had the same nanny for almost thirty years. Her name is Rosa and she is a delightful lady, especially after she has consumed a couple of glasses of wine. She prepared this risotto for me and cheerfully gave me the recipe. It is a luscious dish, and if you can't afford a nanny, make it anyway, and just pretend your nanny cooked it for you.

Note: This is another of those recipes you will (sadly) have to skip if you can't get an important ingredient. If the fresh herbs are not available, skip it. Dry herbs just won't work.

1 tablespoon butter	½ cup fresh sage leaves, finely chopped
2 tablespoons olive oil	
1 medium peeled white onion, thinly sliced	1 quart boiling hot chicken stock
	½ pound mozzarella cheese, shredded
1 large peeled clove garlic, thinly sliced	
	2 tablespoons light cream
1½ cups Arborio rice	Salt and pepper to taste
½ cup dry white wine	2 heaping tablespoons grated Parmesan cheese
½ cup fresh rosemary, leaves only, finely chopped	

Melt butter in oil in a large saucepan on gentle heat. Sauté onion and garlic for eight minutes. Add rice and stir three minutes. Add wine, adjust heat to high, and cook until wine evaporates. Adjust heat to low. Stir in chopped herbs. Add boiling hot broth, cup by cup, constantly stirring, until rice absorbs all the liquid (about eighteen minutes). Stir in mozzarella cheese, the cream, salt and pepper to taste, and grated cheese. Stir vigorously and transfer to deep serving bowl. Bring to table and smile like Rosa.

RECOMMENDED WINES:

RIESLING, GAVI DI GAVI

Risotto del Montanaro

(MOUNTAIN MAN'S RISOTTO)

SERVES 4

This aptly named risotto is redolent of the wild mushrooms found in mountain forests. The men of the mountains of Italy engage in sheep and goat herding and so need food that is calorie-laden to fuel their climbing up steep mountains when leading their flocks to verdant pastures. This is a very hearty risotto that flavorfully supplies the calories required for hard physical labor.

1 ounce dried porcini mushrooms soaked in 1 cup warm water for ½ hour	2 medium potatoes, peeled and diced
1 medium peeled onion, minced	2½ ounces of Italian sweet sausage, skinned and crumbled
1 large peeled clove garlic minced	10 ounces Arborio rice
1 ounce pancetta or bacon, minced	½ cup dry red wine
4 fresh sage leaves, minced	1 quart boiling hot beef stock
1 tablespoon chopped flat leaf parsley	Salt and pepper to taste
3 tablespoons butter	2 tablespoons grated Parmesan cheese
1 clove (the whole clove spice, not powdered)	

Drain the mushrooms through a fine wire sieve lined with a sheet of paper towel. Reserve the liquid for use in soups, stocks, or other risotto. After washing them under cold running water and drying them, chop mushrooms. Set aside.

In a large saucepan on gentle heat, sauté onion, garlic, pancetta, sage, and parsley in two tablespoons of butter for eight minutes. Add clove and cook another two minutes, stirring. Add diced potatoes and stir. Add mushrooms and crumbled

(*continued*)

sausage, stir and cook for fifteen minutes. Add rice, stir, and cook for three minutes. Add wine and cook until it evaporates. Add hot stock, cup by cup, stirring constantly for eighteen minutes until all the liquid has been absorbed by the rice. Add remaining tablespoon of butter, the grated cheese, and mix well. Remove from heat. Remove clove. Let stand covered for four minutes. Pour into a warmed serving bowl and bring to table. Put on a cassette tape of Julie Andrews singing "Climb Every Mountain" and enjoy this outstanding meal.

RECOMMENDED WINES:

BAROLO, NEBBIOLO D'ALBA

Risotto Filante

(STRINGY RISOTTO)

SERVES 4

Filante *translates into "stringiness" and the stringiness comes from the melted mozzarella in the risotto. Mozzarella has that marvelous quality of becoming stringy when melted. Kids young (or old) have fun stretching the strings until they break. This is a sensational risotto for everyone gathered at the family table.*

2 small eggplants, washed, unpeeled, and julienned

5 tablespoons olive oil

Salt and pepper to taste

2-pound 3-ounce can of Italian peeled plum tomatoes, chopped in their liquid

½ peeled chopped onion

1 large peeled clove garlic, thinly sliced

1 rib celery, chopped

¼ cup fresh basil, chopped

Pinch of sugar

11 ounces long-grain rice

1 quart water salted with ½ teaspoon salt

3 tablespoons grated Parmesan cheese

1 pound mozzarella cheese, shredded

In a large skillet, sauté eggplant in olive oil on moderate heat. Season with salt and pepper to taste. Drain in colander, reserving the oil. Set in bowl. Pour drained eggplant oil into a large saucepan and on moderate heat, add tomatoes, onion, garlic, celery, basil, and pinch of sugar. Cook gently for twenty minutes. Set aside. Bring salted water to a boil, stir in rice, cook on a simmer covered for twenty minutes. Drain in colander and set aside. Pour rice into large serving bowl, add diced mozzarella, dress with tomato sauce. Add fried eggplant, mix well, add remaining butter and grated cheese. Stir and serve immediately.

RECOMMENDED WINES:

NERO D'AVOLA, AGLIANICO

Risotto con Calamaretti
(SMALL-SQUID RISOTTO)

SERVES 4

Many American fishing enthusiasts use squid as bait. Not so the Italians. They use succulent squid in dozens of delicious recipes. This is one such recipe, which brings squid to heights of culinary excellence.

1 large peeled white onion, thinly
   sliced

1 large peeled clove garlic, minced

½ cup olive oil

1 cup chopped fresh flat leaf parsley,
   divided in half

15 ounces frozen baby squid
   completely thawed, washed in
   cold water, and julienned

Salt and pepper to taste

1 tablespoon tomato paste dissolved
   in ½ cup dry white wine

1½ cups long-grain rice

1 quart boiling hot fish stock, fresh
   or canned, or clam juice

In a large saucepan, sauté onion and garlic in oil on moderate heat for five minutes. Add first ½ cup chopped parsley, stir, and add squid. Cook for five minutes. Season with salt and pepper. Add tomato paste dissolved in wine and evaporate on high heat three minutes. Lower heat to moderate. Stir in rice, stir, and cook for three minutes. Add hot fish stock or clam juice, cup by cup, until rice absorbs most of the liquid, constantly stirring, for eighteen minutes (it will be a little soupy). Mix in the second ½ cup of parsley. Transfer to serving bowl and bring to table. You'll never use squid for fish bait again. No cheese on fish dishes!

RECOMMENDED WINES:

GRECO DI TUFO, FALANGHINA

Risotto dello Sbirro

(POLICE SPY'S RISOTTO)

SERVES 4

Sbirro *is a contemptuous term for a police spy, or a "narc" in our slang. I was told by one of my relatives in Reggio Calabria, who is a special forces officer in the Italian state police, that this risotto is often the favorite dish of the* sbirri—*the spies—of the area. All I know is that it is very tasty and satisfying. No, it will not transform you into a spy!*

1 tablespoon butter

2 tablespoons olive oil

2 scallions, finely chopped

1 large peeled clove garlic, crushed

1 yellow bell pepper, diced small

1 red bell pepper, pith removed,
   seeded, diced small

1½ cups Arborio rice

Salt and pepper to taste

½ cup dry white wine

1 quart boiling hot chicken stock

1 3½-ounce can tuna packed in oil,
   drained and flaked

½ cup chopped flat leaf parsley

¼ cup chopped fresh basil leaves

In a large saucepan, melt butter in oil on gentle heat. Sauté scallions and garlic for five minutes. Add diced bell peppers, stir, and cook for five minutes. Add rice and stir three minutes. Season with salt and pepper. Add wine and on moderate heat cook until it evaporates. Add hot broth, cup by cup, until rice absorbs all the liquid (about eighteen minutes, constantly stirring). Stir in flaked tuna and chopped herbs. Stir vigorously. Transfer to serving bowl and bring to table. No cheese on fish dishes!

RECOMMENDED WINES:

BIANCO DI SICILIA, GRECO DI TUFO

Risotto con i Carciofi

(ARTICHOKE RISOTTO)

SERVES 4 (WITH A BONUS!)

This is a lovely risotto delicately flavored with artichoke hearts. The original recipe called for four, young, fresh artichokes, all outer leaves removed, and stem cut off, the thistle removed, and pared down to the tender hearts. Then the hearts were julienned and placed into cold water with the juice of one lemon to prevent discoloration. I just don't have the heart to throw away almost all of the artichoke, so I substitute a 14-ounce can of artichoke hearts packed in water. I halve the rest of the artichokes, dip them in egg wash, cover them with bread crumbs seasoned with crushed garlic, chopped parsley, salt and pepper, and grated Pecorino Romano cheese. I fry them in olive oil until golden brown and serve them as appetizers. I did it again, didn't I. I gave you two recipes in one. Oh, well!

2 ounces pancetta or bacon, minced	1 quart boiling hot beef stock
1 cup chopped fresh flat leaf parsley	Salt and pepper to taste
1 large peeled garlic clove, crushed	1½ cups Arborio rice
3 tablespoons butter	2 tablespoons grated Parmesan
4 canned artichoke hearts, julienned	cheese

In a 6-quart saucepan, sauté the pancetta, ½ cup of parsley, and the garlic in two tablespoons of butter on gentle heat for five minutes. Add the artichokes and sauté for three minutes. Add a teaspoon of broth. Season with salt and pepper. Add rice. Stir to heat the grains for five minutes. Add the stock, cup by cup, stirring constantly, until all the broth is absorbed by the rice (about eighteen minutes). Remove from heat. Add one tablespoon of butter, the remaining parsley and the grated cheese. Mix well. Let stand covered for two minutes. Transfer to serving bowl and bring to table. *Proprio gustoso!* (Really delicious!)

RECOMMENDED WINES:

ORVIETO CLASSICO, DOLCETTO D'ALBA

Risotto con Salsiccia e Marsala

(SAUSAGE AND MARSALA WINE RISOTTO)

SERVES 4

Marsala cooking wine is sold in supermarkets. Don't buy it. It is loaded with salt and has only a faint hint of genuine marsala. Please do yourself a favor and buy the real stuff imported from Sicily. Make sure it is dry marsala (secco is the Italian word on the bottle). This is a smashing combination of ingredients that will deliver an excellent risotto. The marsala I use is made by the Florio Company.

2 tablespoons olive oil	1½ cups Arborio rice
1 tablespoon butter	½ cup dry marsala wine
2 scallions, minced	1 quart boiling hot beef stock
3 fresh sage leaves, minced (if you can't get fresh sage, skip it; dried sage simply won't do)	2 tablespoons light cream
	2 tablespoons grated Parmesan cheese
14 ounces Italian sweet sausage, skinned and crumbled	½ cup chopped fresh flat leaf parsley
	Salt and pepper to taste

Heat olive oil and butter in a large saucepan and sauté scallions and sage on gentle heat for eight minutes. Add sausage and fry until well browned, about another eight minutes. Add rice and stir for three minutes. Add marsala wine and cook until completely evaporated. Add hot broth, cup by cup, until all liquid is absorbed by rice (about eighteen minutes). Remove from heat. Stir in cream and grated cheese. Add chopped parsley. Stir. Season with salt and pepper. Pour into warm serving bowl and bring to table. If someone wants more cheese, pass grated Parmesan separately.

RECOMMENDED WINES:

AMARONE, BAROLO

Risotto Povero
(POOR MAN'S RISOTTO)

SERVES 4

The name for this tasty risotto comes from the inexpensive ingredients. Even if you are on a street budget, it doesn't mean you have to eat poorly. When the poor man partakes of this tasty dish, he won't have to sing "If I were a Rich Man," Tevyeh's famous song from Fiddler on the Roof. No it isn't kosher.

½ large onion, minced

3 leaves of fresh sage, minced (if you can't get fresh sage, simply omit it)

1 rib celery, minced

½ cup dry white vermouth

2 tablespoons butter

2 tablespoons olive oil

1½ cups Arborio rice

1 quart boiling hot beef stock

5 ounces mortadella sausage or boiled ham, minced

2 tablespoons grated Parmesan cheese

Ground fresh black pepper to taste

Melt one tablespoon of butter in olive oil in a large saucepan on gentle heat. Add onion, sage (if available), celery, and mortadella. Cook eight minutes. Add rice and stir for three minutes. Add dry vermouth and cook until evaporated. Add the hot beef broth, cup by cup, constantly stirring, until the rice absorbs all the liquid (eighteen minutes). Remove from heat, stir in one tablespoon of butter, grated cheese, and black pepper. Mix well, cover, and let rest two minutes. Pile on a warm serving dish in the form of a little mountain and bring to table. Provide grated Parmesan for those who want it.

RECOMMENDED WINES:

LAMBRUSCO DI GASPAROSSA, DOLCETTO

Risotto con Patate e Zucchine

(POTATO AND ZUCCHINE RISOTTO)

SERVES 4

I *discovered this risotto in the gorgeous city of Ravenna, which is famous for its remarkable mosaics. It was for a time the temporary headquarters of the Holy Roman Emperor Theodoric. If this risotto is an indication of the local cuisine, then its food should be as famous as its mosaics.*

3 medium unpeeled zucchini, washed and diced

2 large potatoes, peeled, diced, and boiled until tender, then drained

1 tablespoon butter

2 tablespoons olive oil

1 large peeled clove garlic, crushed

1 medium peeled onion, minced

1½ cups long-grain rice

½ cup dry white wine

1 quart boiling hot chicken stock

2 tablespoons light cream

2 tablespoons grated Parmesan cheese

¼ cup chopped fresh flat leaf parsley

6 leaves fresh basil, chopped

Salt and pepper to taste

1 walnut-size chunk of cold butter

Melt butter in olive oil in a large saucepan on gentle heat. Add garlic and onion, sauté five minutes. Add potatoes and cook stirring for ten minutes. Add zucchini and cook another five minutes. Add rice, stir for three minutes. Add wine, stir, and as soon as it evaporates add hot broth, cup by cup, until all liquid is absorbed by rice (eighteen minutes). Remove from heat. Incorporate the cream, grated cheese, parsley, and basil. Season with salt and pepper. Stir vigorously, add the cold butter. Cover and let rest for two minutes. Transfer to serving bowl and bring to table. *Saporito!* (Tasty!)

RECOMMENDED WINES:

SOAVE, CHARDONNAY

Risotto della Bella Estate 🦎

(BEAUTIFUL SUMMER RISOTTO)

SERVES 4

Beautiful summers are the seasons for beautiful vegetables. The veggies are at the summit of their color and flavor. I enjoyed this festive risotto while visiting the elegant medieval town of San Gimignano in the verdant hills of Tuscany.

I wrote this recipe in a completely different manner because that is the way the chef who gave me the recipe dictated it to me. I think I like my way of recipe writing better. But you have to admit, it was interesting.

1 large yellow bell pepper
1 large green bell pepper

Wash and dry the peppers. Place them on an outdoor grill and roast them, turning them often, until the skins blister and burn. Place them in a paper bag and close it tightly. Leave them for ten minutes. Remove the peppers. The burned skin can now be easily peeled off. Take out the stems, pith, and seeds. Place the roasted peppers and their juice in a bowl. Set aside.

1 small peeled onion
1 large peeled clove garlic

Mince them and sauté them in a large saucepan, on gentle heat in:

1 tablespoon butter
2 tablespoons olive oil

for five minutes. Add the roasted peppers, large diced, and the pepper juice. Add:

1½ cups Arborio rice

Stir for five minutes. Add:

½ cup dry white wine

and cook over high heat until wine evaporates (about five minutes). Adjust heat to low and add:

4 fresh plum tomatoes processed in food blender for one minute

Stir. Add:

Salt and pepper to taste

Cook, stirring constantly for about eighteen minutes. If rice seems to be getting too dry, add up to two cups of boiling hot chicken broth. Season with:

7 drops Worcestershire sauce

Remove from heat and add:

1 tablespoon butter
½ cup fresh flat leaf parsley, chopped
½ cup fresh basil leaves, julienned

Stir vigorously. Transfer to serving bowl and bring to table. Provide grated Parmesan for those who desire it.

RECOMMENDED WINES:

VERNACCIA DI SAN GIMIGNANO, TREBBIANO

Risotto Esau
(ESAU'S RISOTTO)

SERVES 4

The Old Testament of the Bible tells the story of how Jacob deceived his older brother Esau and tricked him into giving away his birthright as first-born son. Jacob knew his brother Esau was a little dim-witted and was crazy about lentil soup. Esau had just come in from a long, hard day of shepherding his father's sheep and goats. He was famished. Jacob had just finished making lentil soup and told Esau he could eat it all if only he would sign a document. Esau had his lentils and Jacob the birthright of a first-born son. This risotto recipe is about the easiest in the book. All you need is a can opener and the rest will be history.

1 quart boiling hot beef stock	2 tablespoons butter
1 large can (16 ounces) Progresso brand lentil soup	1½ cups Arborio rice
1 medium onion, sliced thinly	2 tablespoons grated Parmesan cheese

Put the broth on to boil. Adjust heat to simmer. Open the can of lentil soup, drain, and reserve the liquid. Add the liquid to the simmering broth. Put a large saucepan on moderate heat, add butter and onion. Sauté onion five minutes. Add rice and stir for three minutes. Add broth, cup by cup, stirring constantly with wooden spoon until rice absorbs all the liquid (about sixteen minutes). Add drained lentils and continue to cook, stirring, for five minutes. Remove from heat. Stir in remaining tablespoon butter and sprinkle with grated cheese. Transfer to serving bowl and bring to table. Don't be like Jacob and tell a lie. Tell everyone the truth. You used a can of lentil soup. They won't believe you anyway. This risotto tastes too darn good.

RECOMMENDED WINES:

VERNACCIA DI SAN GIMIGNANO, ROSSO DI MONTALCINO

Risotto Oktoberfest

(OKTOBERFEST RISOTTO)

SERVES 4

I *traveled to Munich, Germany, several years ago to attend the world-famous Oktoberfest. I never saw so many people in gigantic beer halls drinking huge steins of beer and knocking down knockwurst, bratwurst, sauerkraut, and potatoes. It was a blast! All I could manage to drink was one stein of beer (it held a liter). But you don't have to drink yourself silly to have fun. A few years later I was in Bolzano, Italy. It was Oktoberfest and I saw practically the same scene there as I had in Germany. But this was Italy, after all, and I was served this risotto.*

1 quart boiling hot beef stock	2 tablespoons butter
2 Würstel (Vienna sausages), skinned (Goya is a good brand)	1½ cups Arborio rice
	1 can warm beer (12 ounces)
½ large onion, peeled	¼ cup grated Parmesan cheese

Dice the Vienna sausages. Slice the onion thinly and sauté in one tablespoon of butter in a large saucepan on gentle heat for five minutes. Add rice and stir for three minutes. Adjust heat to high. Add beer and cook until it evaporates. Add hot broth, cup by cup, stirring constantly, until rice absorbs all the liquid (about eighteen minutes). During the last two minutes, add sausage. Stir well. Remove from heat. Stir in remaining tablespoon of butter and grated cheese. A cold glass of beer is the natural accompaniment to this Italian risotto that speaks with a German accent, but I was served a hearty, red wine with my meal. Beer simply blows me up and contains too much sugar for my diabetes.

Risotto Julienne

(JULIENNE'S RISOTTO)

SERVES 4

On my last trip to Reggio Calabria, Sandro La Bozzetta, my compare, took me and my traveling companions Salvatore Vassallo and Frank Di Mauro Jr. to a fabulous country restaurant to celebrate his daughter Claudia's birthday. We traveled in two cars up torturous mountain roads. Mamma Marietta, Sandro, and his wife, Clelia, Claudia, and her fiancé, Sandro Turano, his daughter, Cinzia, and her former fiancé of nine years, Pino Chirico* (whom Cinzia dropped because he had a roving eye). The opening course of my unforgettable culinary family experience was an elegant risotto.

3 tablespoons butter	1½ tablespoons all-purpose flour
2 tablespoons olive oil	½ quart very hot whole milk
1 medium peeled onion, thinly sliced	Salt and pepper to taste
1½ cups Arborio rice	Pinch of nutmeg (⅛ teaspoon)
½ cup dry white wine or dry vermouth	1 pound mozzarella cheese, in small cubes
1 quart boiling hot beef stock	2 ounces boiled ham, julienned
2 tablespoons grated Parmesan cheese	

In a large saucepan, melt 1 tablespoon butter in oil on gentle heat. Sauté onion for five minutes. Add rice and stir three minutes. Add wine and cook until it evaporates. Add hot broth, cup by cup, constantly stirring for eighteen minutes until rice absorbs all the liquid. Add grated cheese. Meanwhile, in another small saucepan, melt 2 tablespoons butter on gentle heat. Stir in flour and cook for three minutes. Add hot milk, constantly stirring until the sauce thickens, about five minutes. You have made béchamel sauce! Season with salt, pepper, and pinch of

---

*While I was writing this book, I received good news from my compare Sandro La Bozzetta concerning his daughter Cinzia. Forget about Pino of the roving eye. She will marry a lieutenant of the Carabinieri (the Italian state police) very soon. Probably by the time this book is published (it takes forever, believe me), she will have had her first child. What's Pino doing? Still looking at every skirt that passes by.

nutmeg. Add mozzarella cubes and stir until cheese melts. Transfer cooked rice into warmed serving bowl. Pour the creamy cheese sauce over the top. Garnish with julienned ham. Bring to table immediately.

RECOMMENDED WINES:

TREBBIANO, SAUVIGNON BLANC

Risotto al Profumo D'Amaretto

(AMARETTO-FLAVORED RISOTTO)

SERVES 4

Amaretto is a delicious liqueur made in Saronno, Italy from bitter almonds. The bitter almonds are also used to make Amaretti di Saronno, very crispy cookies that are great eaten by themselves, and are often used as an ingredient in desserts. They are available in many Italian shops or by mail order (page 5). In this risotto, they give a delightful contrast to the rest of the ingredients.

1 small peeled onion, minced	4 tablespoons light cream
2 tablespoons olive oil	½ teaspoon lemon zest
1½ tablespoons butter	2 Amaretti di Saronno cookies,
1¾ cups Arborio rice	crumbled, or one shot glass of
Salt and pepper to taste	Amaretto liqueur
¼ cup dry white wine or	Pinch of cinnamon
dry vermouth	3 heaping tablespoons grated
36 ounces boiling hot chicken stock	Parmesan cheese

In a large saucepan, sauté onion in oil and butter on gentle heat for five minutes. Add rice and stir for three minutes. Season with salt and pepper. Add wine and cook until completely evaporated. Add hot broth, cup by cup, constantly stirring until the rice absorbs all the liquid (about eighteen minutes). During the last two minutes of cooking, add cream, lemon zest, crushed amaretti, or Amaretto liqueur, and pinch of cinnamon. Remove from heat. Sprinkle with cheese, stir, and serve immediately.

RECOMMENDED WINES:

VERDUZZO, RIESLING

Risotto con Cavolini Bruxelles

(BRUSSELS SPROUTS RISOTTO)

SERVES 4

A *lot of people tell me that they love brussels sprouts but cannot get their kids near them. In this magnificent risotto, the tiny cabbages take on a wonderful taste. Are you having a rough time getting your kids to eat brussels sprouts? Make them this risotto, and unless your kids are really weird, they'll eat them. This is a recipe from the city of Milan.*

2 tablespoons olive oil

1 tablespoon butter

1 tablespoon lard (optional)

1½ tablespoons pancetta or bacon, minced

1 medium peeled onion, thinly sliced

1 large peeled clove garlic, crushed

9 ounces frozen brussels sprouts cooked according to the directions on the package and drained

1½ cups Arborio rice

½ cup dry white wine or dry vermouth

1 quart boiling hot chicken stock

½ cup chopped fresh flat leaf parsley

1 heaping tablespoon grated Parmesan cheese

¼ teaspoon coarsely ground black pepper

Place a large saucepan on gentle heat with oil, butter, and lard, if you are using it. Add onion, brussels sprouts, and garlic. Sauté for five minutes. Add rice and stir. Add wine, adjust heat to high, and cook until wine evaporates (about three minutes). Lower heat to simmer. Add hot broth, cup by cup, constantly stirring, until rice absorbs all the liquid (about eighteen minutes). Remove from heat and vigorously mix in the parsley and grated cheese. Transfer to serving bowl and bring to table. Once in a while you've got to be sneaky to get your kids to eat good things.

RECOMMENDED WINES:

RIESLING ITALICO, VERNACCIA DI SAN GIMIGNANO

Risotto alle Radicchielle
(DANDELION RISOTTO)

SERVES 4

When I was a little child, we had a friend named Donna Micuzza Bareca, who emigrated from Cittanova, a mountain village in the province of Reggio Calabria. Donna Micuzza would often visit Bayonne Park in very early spring and gather the young tender leaves of dandelions, which she always shared with my mother, Donna Carmela. (Donna was the formal title given to women of high station. The English equivalent is "my lady.") The dandelion has a slightly bitter taste and is chock-full of vitamins and minerals. These days you can purchase them from your green grocer or supermarket. This risotto is for you, Donna Micuzza, may you rest in peace.

2 tablespoons butter

2 tablespoons olive oil

1 medium onion, thinly sliced

1½ cups Arborio rice

½ cup dry white wine

1½ pounds dandelion leaves, washed, boiled for five minutes without any more water than that which remains on the leaves from washing, drained, and minced

2 peeled and seeded fresh tomatoes, minced

1 quart boiling hot chicken stock

Salt and pepper to taste

2 tablespoons light cream

2 tablespoons grated Parmesan cheese

Melt 1 tablespoon of butter in olive oil in a large saucepan over gentle heat. Sauté onion for five minutes. Add rice and stir for three minutes. Add wine and cook until evaporated. Add minced dandelions and tomatoes. Cook five minutes. Add hot broth, cup by cup, constantly stirring for eighteen minutes until rice absorbs all liquid. Season with salt and pepper. During the last two minutes of cooking rice, add the cream, the remaining tablespoon of butter, and the grated cheese. Mix well. Remove from the heat, let stand two minutes. Turn into a serving bowl and bring to the table.

RECOMMENDED WINES:

ALCAMO BIANCO, SICILIA VERMENTINO

Risotto Variopinto
(MULTICOLORED RISOTTO)

SERVES 4

This risotto is so colorful and eye-appealing that your guests will whisper when you serve them as if they were visiting an art museum. In fact, I ate this risotto for the first time right around the corner from the Pitti Palace art museum in Florence, Italy. Perhaps the chef was inspired to create his work of art from viewing the magnificent canvases of Rafaello, Tintoretto, El Greco, Goya, and company. This risotto not only looks beautiful but tastes beautiful. What more can one ask?

1 tablespoon butter

2 tablespoons olive oil

1 small peeled onion, thinly sliced

1 large peeled clove garlic, crushed

3 ounces sweet Italian sausage, skinned and crumbled

2 canned Italian plum peeled tomatoes, chopped

2 tablespoons frozen peas, completely thawed

2 frozen artichoke hearts, thawed and julienned

Salt and pepper to taste

1½ cups Arborio rice

½ cup dry white wine or dry vermouth

1 quart boiling hot chicken stock

½ cup chopped fresh flat leaf parsley

1 heaping tablespoon grated Gruyère or Swiss cheese

Melt butter in oil on gentle heat in a large saucepan. Sauté onion and garlic five minutes. Add sausage. Adjust heat to moderate and brown for five minutes. Add tomatoes, peas, and artichokes. Season with salt and pepper and cook, stirring, for ten minutes. Add rice and stir three minutes. Adjust heat to high. Add wine and cook until wine evaporates (five minutes), then lower heat. Add hot stock cup by cup and, with wooden spoon, stir until rice absorbs most of the liquid (about eighteen minutes). Add parsley and grated cheese. Stir vigorously. Remove from heat. Transfer to a deep serving bowl and bring to the table.

RECOMMENDED WINES:

ROSSO DI MONTALCINO, CHIANTI COLLI SENESI

Risi (Rice Dishes)

R*isi* (rice dishes) are recipes where the rice, usually long-grain, is cooked separately and drained. It is combined with the other ingredients in the recipe and then served as is, or baked. But in the following recipe the rice is cooked along with the chicken and vegetables.

Riso alla Pitocca
(BEGGAR WOMEN'S RICE)

SERVES 4 TO 6

A *beggar's life is not easy. Unfortunately, there is a great deal of homelessness in Italy also. This recipe, according to legend, was invented by a poor beggar woman in the middle ages who gathered her alms at the end of the day and with her few pennies bought the ingredients for this dish. She used her imagination and lovingly cooked this magnificent supper for her husband and children.*

1 whole 3-pound chicken with innards

2 carrots

2 medium onions, peeled and left whole

1 large rib celery

1½ quarts water salted with one tablespoon salt

Salt and pepper to taste

1½ cups long-grain rice

2 tablespoons butter

1 cup dry white wine

2 tablespoons grated Parmesan cheese

Wash the chicken well in cold water. Dry it and cut all the meat into bite-size pieces. Remove skin and reserve. Wash the carrots, whole onions, and celery, and place in a large saucepan with the water; bring to a boil. Add the chicken skin, the carcass, and innards, and bring to boil again. Lower heat to simmer and cover for one hour. Strain the broth and put into another pan and keep on simmer for later use. Wash the boiled vegetables and mince them. Place them in a saucepan and cook gently in 1 tablespoon butter for two minutes. Add the chicken pieces and brown lightly (about six minutes). Add wine and cook until evaporated. Season with salt and pepper. Add rice and, stirring, cook for four minutes. Now begin adding the hot chicken broth, cup by cup, stirring constantly for eighteen minutes until the rice has absorbed all the liquid. Remove from heat, mix in remaining tablespoon butter and grated cheese. Serve immediately. That beggar lady sure did know how to cook!

RECOMMENDED WINES:

VERMENTINO, VERDICCHIO

Riso con Filetti di Mandorle

(RICE WITH SLIVERED ALMONDS)

SERVES 4

This rice dish is an interesting combination of contrasting textures and flavors and reminds us of how much we are indebted to the Arab culture. It reflects the Arab invasions in Sicily and Southern Italy. The almonds and raisins are found abounding in North African Arab cuisine.

1 quart water	6 tablespoons milk
11 ounces long-grain rice	½ beef bouillon cube, crushed
1 large peeled onion, sliced thinly	2 ounces slivered almonds
2 tablespoons butter	2 tablespoons olive oil
½ bay leaf	Grated Parmesan cheese to pass at
Salt and pepper to taste	the table
2 tablespoons seedless raisins plumped in warm water for a half hour	

Bring water to boil. Add rice, stir, and cook on moderate heat for twenty minutes. Meanwhile, sauté onion and bay leaf in skillet in butter on gentle heat for eight minutes. Season with salt and pepper. Add raisins, milk, crushed bouillon, and stir. In another small skillet toast the almonds in olive oil on moderate heat until light brown. Add contents of the almond skillet (oil included) to raisin sauce, remove the bay leaf, and stir well. As soon as the rice is cooked, drain it in a colander, pour into serving bowl, toss with sauce, and bring to table. Pass the grated Parmesan cheese. This is an ambrosial main course.

RECOMMENDED WINE:

BIANCO DI ALCAMO (INZOLIA/CATTARRATTO BLEND)

Monticello Giallo di Riso
(LITTLE YELLOW MOUNTAIN OF RICE)

SERVES 4

I *love the imaginative and descriptive names the Italians give to many of their recipes. This "Little Yellow Mountain of Rice" is as delicious as it is pretty. Your kids are going to go off the wall with this one.*

½ quart water

2 beef bouillon cubes

1½ cups long-grain rice

3 fresh egg yolks

2 tablespoons light cream

Pinch of nutmeg

1 tablespoon dry marsala wine

3 tablespoons room-temperature butter, diced

3 tablespoons grated Parmesan cheese

2 hard-boiled egg yolks, grated

In a large saucepan, bring water to boil, crush and drop in bouillon cubes. Sprinkle in the rice. Stir with wooden spoon and cook on moderate heat for eighteen minutes. Remember, keep on stirring. Beat the egg yolks, cream, nutmeg, marsala wine, and diced butter together. Add to the risotto in the last five minutes of cooking. Add the grated cheese. Mix well. Take off heat, cover, and let rest for two minutes. Pour into a serving dish and mold with your spoon into a heaping little mountain. Sprinkle the grated egg yolks over the top and bring to table.

RECOMMENDED WINES:

BARBERA, ROSSO DEL VALTELLINA

Riso in Forma con Salsa Speciale

(BAKED RICE MOLD WITH SPECIAL SAUCE)

SERVES 4

I *tasted this gorgeous baked rice in a resturant in Breuil-Cervinia in the region of Valle D'Aosta, a ski resort town high in the Italian Alps. The majestic Alps were breathtaking and so was this extraordinary riso.*

6 ounces butter

1 peeled onion, thinly sliced

1 leek, trimmed, white bulb only, quartered, washed carefully under cold water, dried, and thinly sliced

1 rib celery, diced small

1 scallion, trimmed of roots, washed, and thinly sliced

10 ounces white cultivated (ordinary) mushrooms, wiped clean with paper towel, and thinly sliced

1 ounce dried porcini mushrooms, softened in a cup of lukewarm water for twenty minutes, washed, dried, and diced

1 beef bouillon cube, crushed

½ cup dry Marsala wine

½ teaspoon coarsely ground black pepper

¼ cup light cream

4 quarts of water with 1 teaspoon salt

1½ cups long-grain rice

2 ounces butter

2 heaping tablespoons grated Parmesan cheese

½ cup chopped fresh flat leaf parsley for garnish

Preheat oven to 350°. Melt 2 ounces butter in a large saucepan on gentle heat. Add onion, leek, celery, and scallion. Sauté eight minutes. Add sliced white mushrooms, stir and cook for three minutes. Add porcini mushrooms. Add crushed bouillion cube. Stir. Add Marsala wine and cook on moderate heat until wine evaporates. Add black pepper. Adjust heat to low and simmer sauce uncovered for thirty minutes. Add cream and stir well, set aside. Meanwhile bring water to boil, stir in rice. Bring back to boil. Cook uncovered for eighteen minutes. Drain rice in colander. Pour into large mixing bowl. Add 2 ounces butter and grated cheese. Stir. Grease an angel food baking pan with last ounces of butter. Press rice mixture into baking pan and bake at 350° for ten minutes. *(continued)*

Pour the mushroom sauce into the bowl of a food processor fitted with a steel blade and process for thirty seconds. If sauce is too dense, mix in a couple of tablespoons of milk, then set aside. Remove rice from oven. Let rest five minutes. Unmold onto a flat serving platter. Cover with sauce. Garnish with chopped parsley.

RECOMMENDED WINES:

PINOT NOIR, LAGREIN

Riso con Uova e Fagiolini
(RICE WITH EGGS AND GREEN BEANS)

SERVES 4

Green beans, I was told by a pink-faced, slim shepherd who was only 97 years old, were so expensive in Italy a century ago, that they were not often found in the cuisine of the common folk. I met Basilo Paternò on the piazza of Rhogudi, a small mountain village inhabited by a few Grecanici (Greek-speaking) families in the province of Reggio Calabria. There were more sheep and goats than people in the piazza that golden November day. I was invited by Basilo to break bread with him and his 50-year-old wife (his second; he married when Filomena, his 70-year-old first wife, died a year ago). Rosinedda was thrilled that this American priest who could speak their dialect was going to write down her recipe.

2 tablespoons butter

1 large clove garlic, left whole (peeled of course)

1½ pounds fresh green beans, washed, ends snapped, boiled in a quart of boiling, lightly salted water for ten minutes, drained and cut into one-inch pieces.

3½ ounces boiled ham, julienned

2 eggs beaten with 2 tablespoons milk

3 tablespoons grated Pecorino Romano cheese

Pinch of salt and pepper

4 quarts water with 1 teaspoon salt

1½ cups long-grain rice

2 egg yolks

2 tablespoons butter

Pinch of nutmeg

Preheat oven to 400°. Place the butter in a large skillet on moderate heat. Add the garlic clove and brown well. Remove the garlic. Add the green beans. Stir and cook for three minutes. Add the julienned ham. Add the eggs beaten with the milk, two tablespoons grated cheese, and seasoned with salt and pepper (she used hot pepper flakes). Scramble in skillet until eggs are set but still moist (about three minutes). Set aside. Bring water to boil in large pot. Stir in rice, allow water to return to boil. Cook the rice fifteen minutes. Drain in colander. Pour into mixing bowl, add two eggs, 1 tablespoon butter, one tablespoon grated cheese, and a pinch

(continued)

of nutmeg. Mix well with wooden spoon. Grease a two-quart angel food cake pan with the last tablespoon of butter. Press in all the seasoned rice. Place in oven for five minutes. Remove, let stand five minutes. Invert on flat serving platter. Fill center with green bean–egg mixture. Serve immediately. Kind of fancy for a country girl, isn't it? Wait until you taste it!

RECOMMENDED WINES:

CIRÒ CLASSICO, NERO D'AVOLA

Tortino di Riso alla Rustica

(PEASANT LADY'S RICE CAKE)

SERVES 4

Peasants throughout the world are known to cook wonderful food with the few foodstuffs they can afford. This rice cake is no exception. It is a very tasty and filling main course. I tasted it for the first time at a weather-beaten wooden table outside a farm shed in the hills surrounding the village of Locri, province of Reggio Calabria in Italy.

3 tablespoons olive oil

2 medium peeled onions, thinly sliced

1-pound can Italian peeled plum tomatoes, and their juice

6 fresh whole basil leaves

1 rib celery, cut in large pieces

3 cloves garlic, peeled and left whole

Salt and pepper

Pinch of sugar

1 beef bouillon cube, crushed

3 tablespoons butter

2 level teaspoons all-purpose flour

1 cup hot milk

3 quarts water with 1 tablespoon salt

10 ounces long-grain rice

1 egg beaten with 2 tablespoons grated Parmesan cheese

1 egg beaten with 2 tablespoons Pecorino Romano cheese

Preheat oven to 350°. In a large skillet, sauté onions in oil on gentle heat for eight minutes. Pour can of tomatoes into skillet and mash with a fork. Add basil, celery, garlic, a pinch each of salt and sugar, and the bouillon. Cook uncovered on moderate heat for twenty minutes. Pour into bowl of a food processor fitted with a steel blade and process for one minute. Reserve sauce. While tomato sauce is cooking. Make a thick béchamel sauce (page 80).

Melt 1 tablespoon of butter in small saucepan. Add flour and stir with wooden spoon on moderate heat for three minutes. Lower heat to simmer and add hot milk. Keep stirring until it becomes very dense (about ten minutes). Remove from heat and season with salt and pepper.

Bring water to boil in 4-quart pot. Stir in rice and bring water back to a boil. Cook rice uncovered for fifteen minutes. Drain in colander. Have two mixing bowls ready. Place half the cooked rice in one and half in the other. Mix one bowl

(continued)

of rice with the béchamel sauce and add mixture of 1 beaten egg and Parmesan cheese.

Mix the second bowl of cooked rice with tomato sauce and the 1 egg beaten with Pecorino Romano cheese.

Grease a bundt pan with 2 tablespoons of butter. Fill the bottom of the pan with the béchamel dressed rice. Press down with a wet spoon. Press in the tomato-dressed rice on top of the bottom layer. Place pan into 350° oven for twenty minutes. Remove, allow to cool for five minutes. Invert onto a flat serving platter and serve immediately.

RECOMMENDED WINES:

CIRÒ CLASSICO, SALICE SALENTINO

Riso in Padella con Prosciutto e Piselli

(PAN-FRIED RICE WITH PROSCIUTTO AND PEAS)

SERVES 4

This fried rice has very little in common with the fried rice from your favorite Chinese take-out shop. It is an exquisite dish and very classy. I sampled this dish in Bergamo, Pope John XXIII's birthplace, in a trattoria (a small family-owned restaurant where the natives go to eat) named Il Buon Papa Giovanni *(Good Pope John). How could I miss?*

2 tablespoons butter	¼ cup boiling hot beef stock
1 large peeled white onion, finely sliced	Salt and pepper to taste
1 tablespoon white lard or fatback, minced (may be omitted)	4 quarts water salted with 1 teaspoon salt
3 ounces prosciutto or boiled ham, julienned	1½ cups long-grain rice
15 ounces fresh peas or frozen, completely thawed	2 tablespoons light cream
	2 heaping tablespoons grated Parmesan cheese

Heat 1 tablespoon butter in a saucepan on gentle heat. Sauté onion and lard if using, for eight minutes. Add julienned prosciutto and cook for five minutes. Add peas and stir for five minutes. Add hot stock. Season with salt and pepper. Cook on moderate heat for ten minutes. Put the mixture into your largest skillet and set aside. Meanwhile, bring water to a boil. Stir in rice and cook uncovered on a boil for eighteen minutes. Drain well in colander. Pour into the skillet into which you placed the peas and prosciutto mixture. On high heat, fry the dressed rice, stirring vigorously with a wooden spoon, for five minutes. Add remaining tablespoon butter and the cream. Stir and remove from heat. Empty into a deep serving bowl, sprinkle grated cheese, and bring to table. Sorry, no fortune cookie with this fried rice!

RECOMMENDED WINES:

BARBERA–BONARDI BLEND, NEBBIOLO

Riso all' Emmental

(SWISS CHEESE RICE)

SERVES 4

This sumptuously rich dish takes about twenty-five minutes to make and is a hearty main course that should be followed by a simple green salad. The nutty flavor of genuine Swiss cheese blends beautifully with the rice. The recipe comes from Lugano, the Italian-speaking town situated in the Ticino Canton of Switzerland.

2 cups rice (any long-grain rice will do)

4 cups water with 1 teaspoon of salt

5 slices Swiss cheese (Emmentaler), diced

1 tablespoon chopped fresh flat leaf parsley

½ cup dry white wine

Pinch of salt

2 medium eggs, beaten

Salt and pepper to taste

Bring water to boil in a large saucepan. Throw in rice, stir, lower heat to simmer, and cook covered for twenty minutes. In another saucepan place diced cheese, butter, parsley, white wine, and a pinch of salt. Cook on low heat stirring continuously until cheese is melted. Add beaten eggs and continue to cook, stirring, for eight minutes. Add the cheese mixture to the rice. Mix well and turn into a warmed bowl. Bring to table.

RECOMMENDED WINES:

MÜLLER THÜRGAU, MERLOT

Riso Pasticciato al Forno

(BAKED RICE PIE)

SERVES 4

The only thing that this tasty dish has in common with what we know as pie is that it's also baked in an oven. No, it is not a dessert. It is a satisfying main course that will have them smacking their lips.

2 cups Arborio or any long-grain rice

2 quarts water with 1 teaspoon of salt

4 tablespoons butter

4 tablespoons grated Parmesan cheese

2 tablespoons grated Gruyère or Swiss cheese

3½ ounces shelled peas, frozen or fresh

½ beef bouillon cube, crushed

5 ounces smoked bacon, coarsely chopped

2 medium eggs, beaten with a pinch of salt

1 tablespoon butter to grease baking dish

Preheat oven to 350°. Boil the rice in the salted water uncovered for fifteen minutes. Drain in colander, pour rice into a bowl, and dress with two tablespoons butter and the cheeses. Mix well. Melt 2 tablespoons butter in small skillet on low heat. Add peas. Dust with a crushed bouillon cube. Cover and cook on lowest heat for fifteen minutes. In another nonstick skillet, sauté bacon on lowest heat just until fat is transparent. Remove bacon and set aside. Now add the beaten eggs to the seasoned, cooked rice. Grease a baking dish with one tablespoon butter. Cover the bottom with a layer of rice, lay on some bacon and another 3 tablespoons of buttered peas, then another layer of rice. Make layers in the same manner until all is used, but end with a layer of rice. Place in preheated 350° oven and bake for fifteen minutes. Bring the dish directly from the oven to the table. (Be careful; put something under the dish or you'll burn the table.)

RECOMMENDED WINES:

VALPOLICELLA, BARBERA D'ASTI

Riso alla Moda del Pioniere

(PIONEER-STYLE RICE)

SERVES 4

*W*here and how this dish got named, I couldn't find out. The only thing I could figure is that anyone who can invent a recipe could be considered a pioneer. Even though I couldn't discover how it was named, it's a very tasty dish.

1½ cups Arborio rice

2 quarts water with 1 teaspoon salt

2 tablespoons butter

2 fresh sage leaves (may be omitted) or use ¼ cup flat leaf parsley on stem

3½ ounces boiled ham, julienned

2 egg yolks

2 tablespoons grated Parmesan cheese

Salt and pepper to taste

¼ cup light cream

Preheat oven to 350°. Cook rice in boiling salted water for twenty minutes. Drain and set aside. In a small skillet, sauté the ham and sage leaves in butter for five minutes on low heat. Discard sage leaves or parsley stem. Beat egg yolks with grated cheese, salt and pepper to taste. Add the seasoning, butter, ham, and beaten eggs to rice. Mix well. Bake in buttered baking dish in 350° oven for fifteen minutes. Let set outside oven for ten minutes. Slice or scoop and serve to your pioneers.

RECOMMENDED WINES:

MERLOT, SANGIOVESE

Riso ai Tanti Sapori

(MANY-FLAVORED RICE)

SERVES 4

The many flavors come from many distinct vegetables and herbs. Yet they are in total harmony with one another and sing in a polyphonic chorus worthy of Palestrina's composition for the Vatican choir. In other words, this terrific rice dish makes your taste buds tingle.

3 tablespoons olive oil

1 small peeled onion, minced

2 scallions, trimmed of root ends, washed, and thinly sliced

1 large peeled clove garlic, minced

2 ounces prosciutto or boiled ham, minced

2 medium carrots, peeled and diced small

2 ribs celery, diced small

1 zucchini, diced small

1 cup chopped flat leaf parsley and basil leaves (equally divided)

¼ cup hot chicken stock

Salt and pepper to taste

¼ teaspoon marjoram

4 quarts water with 1 teaspoon salt

15 ounces long-grain rice

1 tablespoon butter

2 heaping tablespoons grated Parmesan cheese

In a large skillet, sauté onion, scallions, garlic, and prosciutto in oil on gentle heat for eight minutes. Add carrots, celery, zucchini, chopped herbs, and cook slowly, adding stock as needed, for ½ hour. Season with salt, pepper, and marjoram. Meanwhile, bring water to boil in a large pot. Add rice and stir. Cook on the boil, uncovered, for twenty minutes. Drain in colander. Pour into large bowl and mix well with contents of skillet. Add butter and grated cheese. Mix well again. Transfer to deep serving bowl and serve immediately.

RECOMMENDED WINES:

LUGANA DEL VENETO, CHARDONNAY

Riso Degli Arabi ✿

(ARABIAN-STYLE RICE)

SERVES 4

Arabs invaded Sicily many centuries ago and left their distinctive culture, architecture, language, and cuisine. It all became characteristic of Sicily because of the Arab rule over a large part of that island nation. I ate this marvelous dish when I was the guest of the cardinal-archbishop of Palermo, Cardinal Pappalardo. I was sent as a courier for Unico National (an organization of Italian-American business and professional men who engage in raising funds for other charities) to give the cardinal many thousands of dollars to rebuild a large school destroyed by a severe earthquake.

15 ounces long-grain rice	Pinch of salt
2 peeled medium onions, thinly sliced	½ tablespoon cinnamon
4 tablespoons peanut oil or olive oil	¼ teaspoon hot cayenne pepper (powdered)
1 large peeled clove garlic, minced	2 ounces raisins soaked in warm water for ½ hour, drained
1 green bell pepper, roasted, seeded, pith removed, and julienned	Salt and pepper to taste
2½ ounces shelled almonds	

Place the rice in a large pot. Under cold running water, mix with your fingers to release some of the starch. Rinse in a colander. Replace in pot and add cold water two inches above the rice. Bring to a slow boil. Adjust heat to low and simmer covered for fifteen minutes. Meanwhile, sauté the onions in a small skillet in 2 tablespoons of oil on gentle heat for five minutes. Add garlic and roasted pepper and sauté another five minutes. Set aside. In another small skillet, sauté the almonds in the remaining 2 tablespoons of oil on high heat for five minutes. Drain the almonds and cut into slivers. Now add the cinnamon, the cayenne pepper, raisins, and almond slivers to the first skillet. Stir well and empty skillet into cooked rice. Stir vigorously. Transfer to deep serving bowl and bring to table. *Proprio Arabo-Siculo!* (Really Arab-Sicilian!)

RECOMMENDED WINES:

ROSSO DI SICILIA, PRIMITIVO

Budino di Riso con Uova

(RICE PUDDING WITH EGGS)

SERVES 4

Don't let the word "pudding" fool you. This is most definitely not a dessert. Neither is York-shire pudding, for that matter. This is a beautiful baked rice main course that is replete with eggs, parsley, and two kinds of cheese. "'Tis a bonnie puddin, 'tis."

4 quarts water with 1 teaspoon salt

15 ounces long-grain rice

3 tablespoons butter

4 egg yolks

Pinch nutmeg

1 cup fresh flat leaf parsley, chopped

1 heaping tablespoon grated
   Parmesan cheese

1 heaping tablespoon grated Gruyère
   or Swiss cheese

Salt and pepper to taste

2 tablespoons plain breadcrumbs

4 ounces prosciutto or boiled ham,
   julienned

Preheat oven to 350°. Bring water to boil in a 6-quart pan. Stir in rice and return to boil. Cook uncovered for eighteen minutes. Drain rice in colander. Pour into large mixing bowl. Dot with 1½ tablespoons of butter, stir, add egg yolks, pinch of nutmeg, parsley, and grated cheeses. Season with salt and pepper. Stir vigorously.

Grease bundt baking pan with remaining 1½ tablespoons of butter. Dust with breadcrumbs. Spoon in half the cooked rice. Scatter julienned prosciutto. Spoon in remaining rice. Press down with wet spoon. Bake for twenty minutes in 350° oven. Remove and let set for five minutes. Invert onto flat serving platter and serve immediately.

RECOMMENDED WINES:

CHIANTI CLASSICO, BARBERA

Riso e Trippa

(RICE AND TRIPE)

SERVES 4

Tripe is the honeycombed white inside of the cattle's stomach. It is used extensively throughout Europe as an ingredient for soups and main courses. It is a taste I have not acquired, but I include this recipe for the many tripe lovers out there. Enjoy, but please don't ask me to dinner unless you're also making Risotto al Gorgonzola, my favorite.

1 onion, peeled

1 carrot, peeled

1 rib celery

1 garlic clove, peeled

1 fresh rosemary sprig

4 tablespoons olive oil

1 pound fresh tripe, washed very well in salted water, dried, and cut into small ribbon strips

2 quarts boiling hot beef stock

Salt and pepper to taste

1 cup long-grain rice

¼ cup grated Asiago or Parmesan cheese

Put onion, carrot, celery, garlic, and rosemary into bowl of a food processor fitted with a steel blade. Pulse into a coarse mince. Cook the minced vegetables in olive oil in a 6-quart saucepan on gentle heat for five minutes. Add one quart of hot beef stock and tripe. Season with salt and pepper. Cook covered on moderate heat for 1½ hours, stirring often, adding more stock as necessary. Add rest of stock and rice. Cook, always stirring, for twenty minutes. Pour into serving bowl, sprinkle with grated cheese, and serve.

RECOMMENDED WINES:

CHIANTI RISERVA, BRUNELLO DI MONTALCINO

Riso del Lunedì

(MONDAY RICE)

SERVES 4

Why this rice dish is called "Monday Rice" I could never discover. It was served to me by my mamma's godchild, Marietta La Bozzetta, at her home in Reggio Calabria, Italy, on a Sunday afternoon after I had celebrated the noon Mass. I do know it is dramatic in presentation and almost sinfully delectable. I felt that I had to go to confession that evening to Monsignor Caruso at the Casa del Clero where I had my rooms. But after an examination of conscience, I knew that I hadn't committed any sin. This riso *was simply a temptation to commit the sin of gluttony.*

4 tablespoons butter	1 bay leaf
2 tablespoons olive oil	½ teaspoon dry rosemary; crushed
1 large peeled clove garlic, minced	2 tablespoons tomato paste dissolved
2 scallions, trimmed and thinly sliced	in 1 cup hot water
14 ounces hot Italian sausage,	4 quarts water with 1 teaspoon salt
skinned and crumbled	1½ cups long-grain rice
7 ounces very lean beef, julienned	2 heaping tablespoons Pecorino
Salt and pepper to taste	Romano cheese, grated
½ cup dry white wine	Pinch of nutmeg

Preheat oven to 400°. In a large saucepan, melt one tablespoon of butter in oil on gentle heat. Add garlic and scallions and sauté for five minutes. Add the meats seasoned with salt and pepper. Sauté for ten minutes. Add wine and bay leaf. Cook un-

(continued)

til wine evaporates. Add the tomato paste dissolved in hot water. Cover and simmer for thirty minutes. Remove bay leaf and stir in rosemary. Meanwhile, bring water to boil. Add rice and cook uncovered at a boil for twenty minutes. Drain the rice and pour into a bowl. Add 1 tablespoon of butter, a tablespoon of grated cheese, and a pinch of nutmeg and stir vigorously with a wooden spoon. Grease a bundt baking pan with the last 2 tablespoons of butter. Place ¾ of the cooked rice in bottom of baking pan. Press down the rice and make a large dent in the center. Fill the center with the meat sauce. Sprinkle with remaining grated cheese. Cover with remaining rice. Press down. Place bundt baking pan in preheated 400° oven for ten minutes. Remove. Let rest five minutes. Unmold by turning upside down on serving platter and bring to table. One taste and you'll want Monday Rice on any day. *Magnifico!* (Magnificent!)

RECOMMENDED WINES:

CHIANTI CLASSICO, VINO NOBILE DI MONTEPULCIANO

Riso con Salsa allo Zafferano

(RICE WITH SAFFRON SAUCE)

SERVES 4

Saffron is probably the world's most expensive spice, at two thousand dollars a pound. It is the stigma of a crocus flower that must be removed by hand. It is also probably the most exquisite spice in the world. I use Badia saffron at $2.49 a package. That contains 0.4 gram. This minuscule amount is enough to beautifully color and flavor most dishes. There are imitations available, but please use genuine saffron. It is worth it.

4 quarts water with 1 tablespoon salt

11 ounces Arborio rice

¼ cup dry white wine

2 scallions, finely chopped

3 white peppercorns

2 tablespoons butter

4 tablespoons minced carrot, onion, celery

1 slice prosciutto or boiled ham

1 tablespoon all-purpose flour

2 small packages Badia saffron (0.4 gram each) dissolved in 1 cup hot beef stock

4 tablespoons grated Parmesan cheese

Bring water to a boil. Add rice and cook on moderate heat for twenty minutes. Drain in colander and reserve. For wine sauce:

In a small saucepan, place wine, scallions, and peppercorns on low heat, reduce until half the wine is evaporated. Press contents through food mill or place in a blender and pulse until smooth. Reserve.

In a large saucepan, sauté 4 tablespoons of minced vegetables and ham in butter on gentle heat for five minutes. Sprinkle in flour and stir until flour has turned light brown in color. Add saffron dissolved in hot stock. Cook on low heat for fifteen minutes. Pour cooked rice into a bowl with wine and saffron sauces. Mix and sprinkle with grated cheese. Turn upside down on serving platter and bring to table. Whew! Complicated isn't it? But it's well worth the effort. I enjoyed this dish at an outdoor restaurant in Milan.

RECOMMENDED WINES:

BARBARESCO, BARBERA

Riso del Barcaiolo

(BOATMAN'S RICE)

SERVES 4

Boatmen eat fish, don't they? Obviously, this dish was named in recognition of that fact. The fish is canned tuna, so we don't have to venture onto a boat to net our catch. I'm glad about that, because I'm prone to motion sickness on small boats. So, whoever invented this recipe did people like me a big favor. Besides that, this riso *dish is very palatable (that means yummy).*

1 tablespoon butter	1 6-ounce can tuna packed in olive
2 tablespoons olive oil	oil, drained and flaked
1 medium peeled onion, small diced	½ cup fresh flat leaf parsley, chopped
1 beef bouillon cube, crushed	½ cup fresh basil leaves, chopped
Salt and pepper to taste	4 cups water with ½ teaspoon salt
½ cup dry white wine	2 cups long-grain rice
1 cup hot water	

In skillet sauté onion in butter and oil on gentle heat ten minutes. Sprinkle crushed bouillon over it and season with salt and pepper. Add wine and cook until it evaporates. Add hot water 2 teaspoons at a time if onions get too dry. Cook five more minutes. Add tuna, parsley, basil, and remaining hot water. Stir and set aside. Meanwhile, bring 4 cups salted water to boil. Add rice and stir. Adjust heat to low and simmer for twenty minutes, covered. Pour rice into serving bowl, dress with onion-tuna sauce, mixing well. Bring to table. Do not serve cheese with any kind of fish.

RECOMMENDED WINES:

CHARDONNAY, ARNEIS

Riso con Uova e Cavolfiore

(RICE WITH EGGS AND CAULIFLOWER)

SERVES 4

Cauliflower belongs to the cruciferous family of vegetables, along with broccoli. The crucifers are recommended by the medical community as a natural preventative for stomach and intestinal cancers. Cauliflower by itself is a rather bland vegetable but combined with other ingredients, it has the wonderful ability to absorb their flavors. This rice recipe transforms cauliflower into a tantalizing vegetable. Nothing drab or bland about it.

1 medium cauliflower	Salt and pepper to taste
4 quarts water with 1 tablespoon salt	1 tablespoon chopped fresh flat leaf parsley
1 medium peeled onion, thinly sliced	
3 tablespoons butter	11 ounces long-grain rice
2 large eggs	2 ounces grated Gruyère or Swiss cheese
2 tablespoons milk	

Bring salted water to boil. Cut off outer leaves and core of cauliflower and place in boiling water. Cover and cook for ten minutes. Drain in colander, reserve water, allow to cool, and break into flowerettes. Set aside. In large skillet, sauté onion in butter for five minutes. Add cauliflower, mix well and remove from heat. In a large saucepan, bring reserved water to boil and add rice, stir, and cook on moderate heat for twenty minutes. Drain in colander. Pour into serving bowl and add cooked cauliflower. Beat eggs with milk and seasoning. Pour into rice. Stir in parsley. Sprinkle with grated cheese, stir and bring to table.

RECOMMENDED WINES:

TOCAI FRIULANO, SOAVE

Riso Gratinato con Funghi e Fegatini

(CRUSTY BAKED RICE WITH MUSHROOMS AND CHICKEN LIVERS)

SERVES 4

This is such a pretty and tantalizing dish. The first time I tasted it was at the home of Franco La Bozzetta, Marietta's oldest son, who lives on the outskirts of Catania, Sicily. I'm not partial to chicken livers, but this preparation was so outstanding, I actually relished them.

2 tablespoons olive oil

1 tablespoon pancetta or bacon, minced

1 peeled medium onion, minced

1 large peeled clove garlic, minced

½ peeled carrot, minced

1 rib celery, minced

4 fresh sage leaves, minced or ¼ teaspoon dried

7 ounces cleaned chicken livers, minced

10 ounces ordinary mushrooms, sliced

Salt and pepper to taste

2 tablespoons cognac

1 tablespoon tomato paste dissolved in ½ cup dry white wine

2 tablespoons light cream

4 quarts water with 1 teaspoon salt

1½ cups long-grain rice

4 tablespoons butter

1 tablespoon grated Gruyère or Swiss cheese

Plain bread crumbs

Preheat oven to 400°. In a large saucepan, heat oil on moderate heat. Sauté onion and garlic five minutes. Add carrot, celery, and sage. Sauté eight minutes. Add chicken livers. Sauté five minutes. Add sliced mushrooms and sauté ten minutes. Season with salt and pepper. Add cognac and cook on high heat until it evaporates (about three minutes). Add tomato paste dissolved in wine. Lower heat and cook

uncovered for twenty minutes. Meanwhile, bring water to boil. Stir in rice and one tablespoon of butter. Boil uncovered for fifteen minutes. Drain and pour into bowl. Add 1 tablespoon of butter and grated cheese. Mix well. Grease an angel food cake pan with 1 tablespoon of butter. Dust with bread crumbs. Press cooked rice into the pan with a wet spoon. Dust top of rice with 2 tablespoons of bread crumbs and dot with last tablespoon of butter. Bake in preheated 400° oven for twenty minutes. Remove and let cool for ten minutes. Unmold on serving platter. Fill center with chicken liver-mushroom sauce. Bring to table. *Elegante!* (Elegant!)

RECOMMENDED WINES:

BARBERA D'ALBA, NERO D'AVOLA

Riso del re Sole

(RICE OF THE SUN KING)

SERVES 4

They don't call it sunny Italy for nothing. The sun is king! Without it, nothing would grow. Life, as we know it, would not exist if the sun were extinguished. This is the culinary version of the famous hymn to the sun, "O Sole Mio." Scientists tell us that millions of humans suffer depression as a result of deprivation of sunlight. This riso is a natural antidepressant with no unpleasant side effects. Feeling blue? Make and eat this sunny riso.

3 quarts water with 1 teaspoon salt

11 ounces long-grain rice

2 tablespoons butter

10 ounces frozen spinach, cooked according to package directions, squeezed dry, and chopped finely

4 tablespoons frozen peas, thawed, cooked for 5 minutes in boiling water and drained

20 ounces (1¼ pounds) sweet Italian sausage, skinned, crumbled, and browned well in:

1 tablespoon olive oil in large deep skillet

2 tablespoons light cream

2 tablespoons grated Parmesan cheese

2 teaspoons coarsely ground black pepper

Bring water to boil in a saucepan, stir in rice, and cook, covered, on gentle heat for twenty minutes. Stir in 1 tablespoon of butter. Pour into a bowl. Cook spinach and peas according to directions in ingredient list. Cook sausage according to direction in ingredient list. Add butter to skillet in which you cooked sausage, stir, add spinach and peas, and cook for five more minutes. Add rice, cream, grated cheese, and ground black pepper. Mix well and transfer to serving bowl. Bring to table and eat while Pavarotti sings "O Sole Mio" on your stereo. This will chase your blues away. Guaranteed!

RECOMMENDED WINES:

CHIANTI CLASSICO, MORELLINO DI SCANSANO

Riso con Peperoni e Peperoncino
(RICE WITH SWEET AND HOT PEPPERS)

SERVES 4

This is an astounding rice dish combining the natural sweetness of bell peppers with the bite of hot peppers. I find it delightful and satisfying, but I only make it when the grocers' or supermarkets' vegetable bins are selling bell peppers in season. I simply refuse to buy produce out of season and pay outrageous prices. Besides, all vegetables are best when in season because they are at the peak of their flavor and texture.

1 tablespoon butter	6 tablespoons canned tomato sauce
2 tablespoons olive oil	1 large jalapeño pepper, chopped with seeds
20 ounces (1¼ pounds) altogether of green, red, and yellow bell peppers, pithed, seeded, and julienned	Salt and pepper to taste
	1 quart boiling hot chicken stock
	12 ounces long-grain rice
1 medium peeled onion, thinly sliced	2 hard-boiled eggs

In a large saucepan, sauté the bell peppers, onion, tomato sauce, and hot pepper in butter and olive oil on moderate heat. Season with salt and pepper. Cover and cook for ½ hour. Set aside. Meanwhile bring broth to boil, add rice, and simmer for fifteen minutes, stirring constantly until the rice absorbs the liquid completely. Add cooked rice to cooked pepper mixture. Mix well. Garnish with hard-boiled egg slices after filling serving bowl with rice and pepper sauce. Serve immediately.

RECOMMENDED WINES:

ROSSO DI SICILIA, SALICE SALENTINO

Riso dell' Alpino

(ALPINE RICE)

SERVES 4

The Italian Alps are studded with quaint villages where the food is hardy and phenomenal. The inhabitants need plenty of calories to sustain them in the cool mountain air while they engage in hard work. Just walking uphill is hard work for me when I visit their gorgeous towns. Charles Atlas (an Italian, by the way) I am not.

2 tablespoons butter	1 shot glass cognac
1½ ounces pancetta or bacon, minced	1½ cups long-grain rice
1 large peeled clove garlic, minced	1 quart boiling hot beef stock
½ large peeled white onion, diced	3 tablespoons grated Parmesan
¼ teaspoon dried sage	cheese
1 rib celery, diced small	
9 ounces sweet or hot Italian sausage,	
skinned and crumbled	

Melt one tablespoon of butter on moderate heat in a large saucepan. Add pancetta, garlic, onion, sage, and sausage. Sauté for ten minutes on low heat. Add cognac. Adjust heat to high and cook for three minutes. Add rice and stir for three minutes. Adjust heat to moderate. Add hot broth and stir constantly for fifteen minutes. Remove from heat. Add remaining tablespoon of butter and grated cheese. Stir briskly and serve immediately. You may keep grated Parmesan cheese on hand for those who want it.

RECOMMENDED WINES:

VALPOLICELLA, BARBERA D'ALBA

Riso con Salsa di Cipolle

(RICE WITH ONION SAUCE)

SERVES 4

Onions and garlic are in the same botanical family as lilies. I can get along without lilies until the day they lay me out, but I can hardly cook without onions and garlic. This is a delightful rice dish because the onions cook until they are deep brown and release their natural sweetness. And no one will approach you and say, "Phew—you were eating onions, I can smell you from a mile away!" Only eating raw onions may cause that kind of reaction. Eat and enjoy. Pop a Tic-Tac into your mouth if you're worried. (Tic-Tacs are made in Italy.)

2 quarts water with 1 teaspoon salt	1 level tablespoon all-purpose flour
1½ cups long-grain rice	¾ cup hot chicken stock
4 medium peeled onions, thinly sliced	6 tablespoons light cream
3 tablespoons butter	Pinch of nutmeg
Salt and pepper to taste	2 tablespoons grated Parmesan cheese
¼ cup dry white wine	

Boil the rice uncovered in salted water for twenty minutes. Meanwhile, sauté the onions on gentle heat in 2 tablespoons of butter in a saucepan. Cook until very brown (caramelized). Season with salt and pepper. Add wine and cook until completely evaporated. Sprinkle with flour, stir and cook five more minutes. Add chicken broth and stir to liquefy the sauce (three minutes). Simmer for fifteen minutes. Empty into food blender, add the cream and pinch of nutmeg. Blend for one minute. When the rice is cooked, drain in colander. Empty into a preheated serving bowl. Stir in the onion sauce, the remaining tablespoon of butter, and the grated cheese. Stir well and bring to table.

RECOMMENDED WINES:

GATTINARA, BARBERA

Riso alla Salsa di Avocado

(RICE WITH AVOCADO SAUCE)

SERVES 4

I tasted this unusual rice *in the singular and beautiful city of Perugia. Perugia is the capital of the region of Umbria, and it is built on the ruins of two other cities; the first, Etruscan, the second, Roman. A series of escalators bring you to the historic center and the Via Fanucci, a pedestrian mall leading to the cathedral. While I visited the cathedral, I was witness to an incident. An elderly priest stopped a woman wearing a modest short sleeve blouse. He said loudly, "What is this place? A zoo for naked beasts, or is it the house of God?" I felt sorry for the embarrassed woman and for the elderly priest. I prayed for them both.*

4 quarts water with 1 teaspoon of salt

1½ cups long-grain rice

2 hard-boiled egg yolks, grated

1 tablespoon butter, at room temperature

2 large avocados, pitted, flesh scooped out with a spoon, and cut into small pieces

½ lemon, juiced

Salt and pepper to taste

¼ cup chopped fresh basil leaves

½ cup whipped cream (no sugar)

Cook the rice in boiling water, uncovered, for twenty minutes. Meanwhile, beat together the butter and egg yolks. Add avocado and whip with a whisk. Add lemon juice, season with salt and pepper, and add basil. Whip vigorously to homogenize the mixture. Fold in the whipped cream. Fold into cooked, drained rice. This delicately flavored *riso* doesn't need any grated cheese.

RECOMMENDED WINES:

TOCAI FRIULANO, TREBBIANO, OR MALVASIA

Riso al Forno del Norcino

(NORCIA-STYLE BAKED RICE)

SERVES 4

Norcia is a small town located in the region of Umbria. Umbria is still a heavily forested area, and innumerable mushrooms grow from the decaying vegetation on its forests' floors. Many recipes, including this one, containing lovely mushrooms, are designated alla Norcina, or del Norcino, because Norcia grows some of the best wild mushrooms in Italy.

½ large peeled white onion, thinly
    sliced

3 tablespoons butter

1 ounce dried porcini mushrooms,
    soaked in 1 cup warm water for
    ½ hour, drained and liquid
    carefully strained and reserved.
    Chop mushrooms.

6 ounces Italian sweet sausage,
    skinned and crumbled

½ package frozen peas, thawed

2 canned or frozen artichoke hearts,
    julienned

1 beef bouillon cube, crushed

4 cups water with 1 teaspoon salt

1 tablespoon dry white wine

2 heaping tablespoons grated
    Parmesan cheese

Preheat oven to 400°. In a large saucepan, sauté onion in 2 tablespoons of butter for five minutes. Add mushrooms, sausage, peas, artichokes, bouillon, and strained mushroom liquid. Cook gently on low heat for ½ hour. Meantime, boil rice in four cups of water for five minutes. Drain quickly so rice will still be watery. Add wet rice to the saucepan. Add wine, 1 tablespoon of butter, and grated cheese. Mix well. Pour rice mixture into a baking dish (with cover) and bake covered for ten minutes. Remove cover and continue to bake until a light, golden crust begins to form, about ten more minutes. Remove from oven and serve immediately.

RECOMMENDED WINES:

VINO NOBILE DI MONTEPULCIANO, SAGRANTINO DI MONTEFALCO

Riso San Remo

(SAN REMO RICE)

SERVES 4

San Remo is on the Italian Riviera in the region of Liguria. It is a pricey and trendy seaside resort where the beautiful people gather to see and be seen. They don't check your passport in this town, they check your bank accounts. I wandered away from the topless beach to the back streets where the natives live. I found a tiny trattoria (family-run restaurant) where the menu was memorized by the fourteen-year-old daughter of the owner. Alessandra suggested this dish. I was delighted with the food and even more delighted to pay seven dollars for a complete meal, including a liter of homemade wine. You don't have to go broke to eat gourmet food.

2 tablespoons butter, melted	1 cup homemade cubes of stale
1½ cups Arborio rice	Italian bread fried in olive oil
¼ cup dry white wine	(croutons)
1 quart boiling hot chicken stock	½ pound fontina cheese, cubed
Pinch of cinnamon	

Preheat oven to 450°. In a large saucepan, add 1 tablespoon of melted butter and on moderate heat, cook rice for three minutes, stirring. Add wine and cook until it evaporates. Stir vigorously so the rice doesn't stick. Add hot broth, cup by cup, until all the liquid is absorbed by the rice (about eighteen minutes). During the last two minutes of stirring constantly, add cinnamon. Pour into a baking dish that can be brought to the table, first a layer of rice sprinkled with half the croutons and half the cheese. Add another layer of rice and end with the remaining croutons and cheese. Drizzle with remaining melted butter. Place in oven for ten minutes. Remove and serve.

RECOMMENDED WINES:

CINQUETERRE (WHITE), VERMENTINO DI SARDINIA

Sformato di Riso con le Uova

(RICE MOLD WITH EGGS)

SERVES 4

This dish makes such a spectacular presentation that you don't know whether to take its photograph or eat it. I was faced with this dilemma when Clelia La Bozzetta brought it to our dinner table. I solved the problem. I took its photo and dug into it without mercy. Boy, is this awesome!

2 quarts water with 1 teaspoon salt	10 ounces tomato sauce, canned or
1 cup long-grain rice	fresh
1 large green bell pepper, pithed,	4 fresh large eggs at room
seeded, and cut into strips	temperature
1 tablespoon butter	5 tablespoons olive oil
Salt and pepper to taste	Salt and pepper to taste

Bring salted water to boil. Add rice, stir, and adjust heat to moderate. Cook rice uncovered for twenty minutes. Drain well. Pour into a well-greased ring mold. Sauté pepper strips in skillet in butter on moderate heat for eight minutes. Season with salt and pepper. Add the tomato sauce and cook on low heat for ten minutes. Set aside but keep warm. In another skillet, fry the eggs sunny-side up, or as they say in Italian, *all' occhio di bue* (ox eyes), on high heat for four minutes. Season with salt and pepper. Unmold rice onto a platter (it's okay if it falls apart, just shape it into a ring). Arrange the cooked eggs around the outside crown of the rice and pour the tomato sauce and place the cooked pepper strips in the center of the ring of rice. What a beauty!

RECOMMENDED WINES:

PINOT NOIR/NERO, TEROLDEGO

Riso al Forno Villa San Giovanni

(BAKED RICE VILLA SAN GIOVANNI)

SERVES 4

Villa San Giovanni is the major port of embarkment to Sicily from the Italian mainland. It is in the province of Reggio Calabria. The huge ferries transport trains, trucks, cars, and of course people from Italy to Messina, Sicily. A short distance from the busy port, the town climbs a gentle slope of a mountain, and is a beautiful gem of a village completely rebuilt after the terrible earthquake and tidal wave of 1908. Anyway, this is a sumptuous dish that will please everyone in the house.

1 quart water

4 tablespoons olive oil

½ peeled large onion, sliced thinly

1 large peeled clove garlic, crushed

3 large ripe tomatoes, chopped

1 tablespoon chopped flat leaf parsley

1¾ cups long-grain rice

Salt and pepper to taste

¼ cup grated Pecorino Romano cheese (we're back in Southern Italy)

1 10-ounce package frozen peas, completely thawed

3½ ounces prosciutto or boiled ham, chopped

5 ounces Italian sweet sausage, skinned and crumbled

2 hard-boiled eggs

12 black pitted olives, sliced in rings

1 fresh egg yolk

2 tablespoons milk

2 tablespoons butter, diced

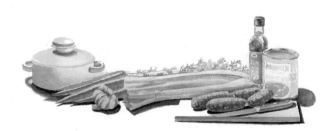

Preheat oven to 375°. Bring the water to a boil in a saucepan. Meantime, in another large saucepan, sauté onion and garlic in olive oil on moderate heat for five minutes. Add chopped tomatoes. Cook for ten minutes. Add parsley and rice. Season with salt and pepper, mix well, and add the boiling hot water all at once. Cook, stirring continuously, for eighteen minutes. Cover and set aside. Butter a baking dish and place a layer of rice to cover bottom. Cover with thawed peas, sprinkle with chopped prosciutto, and crumbled sausage (yes, that is right, uncooked). Cut hard-boiled eggs into slices and distribute evenly over the layer of the remaining rice. Beat the egg yolk with the milk and pour over the top. Dot with butter. Place in preheated oven for fifteen minutes. Remove, let rest for five minutes. Serve immediately.

RECOMMENDED WINES:

CIRÒ RISERVA, SALICE SALENTINO

Tortino di Riso al Verde

(GREEN RICE TART)

SERVES 4

Mantova is the home of this attractive rice tart. It was also the home of the great Latin poet, Virgil. Virgil wrote the epic poem, The Aeneid, the legendary story of Aeneas, who vies in legend with Romulus and Remus as the founder of Rome. Today, Mantova's historical center is a remarkably preserved medieval town. Its cuisine is also famous for Gnocchi al Gorgonzola and Pasta Strazzopreti (these are found in my previous books.)

4 tablespoons butter	Pinch of nutmeg
1 peeled clove garlic, crushed	3 egg yolks
1 package frozen spinach, completely thawed	2 tablespoons light cream
	1 tablespoon grated Parmesan cheese
Salt and pepper to taste	1 tablespoon grated Gruyère or Swiss cheese
1 chicken bouillon cube, crushed	
2 quarts water with 1 teaspoon salt	2 heaping tablespoons plain bread crumbs
1½ cups long-grain rice	

Preheat the oven to 350°. Melt 1 tablespoon of butter in skillet on gentle heat. Add garlic and sauté five minutes. Add spinach, cover, and cook for ten minutes. Season with salt and pepper, and crushed bouillon. Let cool. Bring water to boil. Add rice, stir, and cook uncovered for twenty minutes. Drain in colander. Finely chop spinach when still warm. Pour into a bowl, dress with 1 tablespoon butter and pinch of nutmeg. Add one egg yolk at a time and beat after each addition. Beat in cream and grated cheese. Butter a springform cake pan with 1 tablespoon of butter. Sprinkle bottom and sides with bread crumbs. Add rice and spinach. Mix well. Level off and press down with a wet spoon. Dot with last tablespoon of butter. Place in preheated oven and bake for forty minutes. Cool for ten minutes. Remove sides of springform pan. Bring to table and slice in generous portions to serve.

RECOMMENDED WINES:

BARBERA D'ALBA, NEBBIOLO D'ALBA

Riso al Pomodoro

(TOMATO SAUCED RICE)

SERVES 4

This is a simply delicious main course or a great side dish to accompany roasts, chops, cutlets, or poultry. It is a nice change, as a side dish, from the usual fried or baked potatoes.

4 quarts water with 1 tablespoon salt

2 cups long-grain rice

1 tablespoon olive oil

1 tablespoon butter

1 large peeled clove garlic

1 1-pound can Italian plum peeled tomatoes with their juice

Pinch of salt and ½ teaspoon hot pepper flakes

½ cup chopped fresh flat leaf parsley

½ cup washed whole fresh basil leaves packed down

Put water on to boil in 6-quart saucepan. Stir in rice and boil uncovered ten minutes. Drain and reserve. Meanwhile, in a large deep skillet, sauté garlic clove in oil and butter on moderate heat until garlic is golden brown. Discard garlic (give it to me to spread on my slice of toasted Italian bread). Add contents of canned tomatoes, mash tomatoes with a fork, add salt and hot pepper. Bring to boil. Add reserved rice. Stir constantly for ten minutes on moderate heat. Stir in parsley and basil. Remove from heat. Cover and let rest two minutes. Pour into warmed serving bowl and bring to table. Provide Pecorino Romano cheese to pass at table.

RECOMMENDED WINES:

CANNONAU DI SARDEGNA, SANGIOVESE

Riso al Forno alla Marietta

(MARIETTA'S BAKED RICE)

SERVES 6

My surrogate mother, Marietta La Bozzetta, of Reggio Calabria, Italy, was 92 years young, when she died last year. She was so dear to me because she was my deceased mamma's godchild. When she cooked, watch out! Her Riso Al Forno would feed an army. This is a heavy yet heavenly dish.

2 large peeled white onions, thinly sliced

¼ cup butter

¼ cup olive oil

3 cups long-grain rice

6 cups skim milk

2 chicken bouillon cubes, crumbled

¼ teaspoon powdered saffron

½ cup grated Pecorino Romano cheese

1 pound mozzarella cheese, cubed

1 pound domestic provolone cheese, cubed

1 pound hot or sweet Italian sausage, skinned, crumbled, and browned very brown in a skillet, then drained of grease on paper towels

1 ounce dried porcini mushrooms soaked in warm water ½ hour, drained, washed well under cold running water, dried and chopped

Preheat oven to 350°. In a very large saucepan, sauté onion in butter and oil on moderate heat for five minutes. Add rice and stir three minutes. Add milk, crushed bouillon, and saffron. Cook on gentle heat (after the milk has come to a boil) for eight minutes, constantly stirring. The rice will absorb most of the liquid. Heavily grease a large baking dish. Spoon in a layer of cooked rice on the bottom of pan. Sprinkle with cooked sausage, grated cheese, mozzarella, and provolone cubes, and chopped mushrooms. Keep layering in this manner, winding up with a layer of rice sprinkled with remaining grated cheese. Cover with aluminum foil tightly. Bake 30 minutes. Remove foil and bake eight more minutes. Remove from oven. Let set for five minutes, cut, and serve. *Mamma Mia!*

RECOMMENDED WINES:

AGLIANICO, PRIMITIVO

Riso alla Malesiana

(MALAYSIAN RICE)

SERVES 4

Malaysian rice! In an Italian cookbook! Now, calm down. There is an explanation. My compare *Sandro La Bozzetta* and his wife *Clelia* traveled to Egypt on an Italian cruise ship. The second day on board they were served this "Malaysian" rice. They loved it. But Clelia, nifty lady that she is, asked to speak to the chef. He was an Italian from the island of Ischia in the Bay of Naples. Clelia asked him where did the name of this dish originate. He smiled and said: "I made it up. I thought it sounded exotically oriental." So, that's the story.

1 cup long grain-rice

4 cups water with 1 teaspoon salt

1 large peeled onion

8 ounces boiled beef (round steak)

1 large bell pepper, green, yellow, or
    red, pithed and seeded

6 tablespoons olive oil

2 large eggs, beaten

Salt and pepper to taste

Boil rice uncovered in salted water for fifteen minutes. Drain and reserve. Meanwhile, slice the onion thinly. Dice the boiled beef and cut the seeded bell pepper into about one-inch squares. In a large skillet, brown the onion in 4 tablespoons of olive oil on low heat. Remove with slotted spoon. In same oil, brown the meat and remove with slotted spoon. Sauté the pepper squares in same oil for eight minutes. Remove with slotted spoon. Put all the sautéed ingredients in a bowl. In the same skillet, fry the beaten eggs on low heat, beating with a fork until they firm up but are still moist. Pour eggs into a bowl. To the same skillet, add 2 remaining tablespoons of olive oil. As soon as it is hot, add the boiled rice, the cooked onion, beef, bell peppers, and eggs. Season with salt and pepper. On moderate heat, stir to amalgamate all the ingredients. Remove from heat. Let rest for two minutes, then pour into serving dish. Bring to table. This dish is about as Malaysian as Luciano Pavarotti!

RECOMMENDED WINES:

NEBBIOLO, TEROLDEGO ROTILIANO

Riso e Verze con Salsicci
(RICE WITH SAVOY CABBAGE AND SAUSAGES)

SERVES 4

Savoy cabbage has distinctive, wrinkled green leaves and more flavor than ordinary head cabbage. It's a natural when combined with Italian sausage. When you purchase Italian sausage, make sure it is very lean (more red meat than ground white pork fat). Check the ingredients. It must be seasoned with fennel seeds. This is a spicy rice dish that everyone will enjoy.

1 large head savoy cabbage

1½ ounces pancetta or unsmoked bacon

1 teaspoon dry rosemary crushed into a powder

1 large peeled garlic clove

3 tablespoons olive oil

1 cup long-grain rice

1 quart boiling hot chicken stock

4 links Italian sausage, sweet or hot, skinned

4 heaping tablespoons grated Parmesan cheese

Tear off all the leaves of the cabbage. Discard any outer, withered leaves. Wash well in cold water, drain and chop coarsely. Julienne the pancetta. Mince the rosemary with garlic. In a large saucepan, fry the pancetta in oil for eight minutes on moderate heat. Add the cabbage, cover and cook for eight minutes on low heat. Add minced rosemary and garlic. Add rice. Stir three minutes. Add the broth and bring to boil on high heat. At the same time, fry the skinned sausages in a nonstick skillet until well browned all over, at least twelve minutes. Try to keep the sausages whole. Transfer the cooked sausages to the boiling soup. Lower heat to low and simmer for ten minutes. Remove sausages with slotted spoon. Transfer soup into tureen. Sprinkle cheese. Serve in individual soup bowls, topping each with a sausage. *Molto buono!* (Very good!)

RECOMMENDED WINES:

SCHIOPETTINO, BARBERA

Riso Nettuno

(NEPTUNE'S RICE)

SERVES 4

Neptune was the Roman god of the seas. Since this recipe calls for tuna fish, someone who knows Roman mythology baptized it Neptune's Rice. I think it makes sense, don't you?

16 white pearl onions (small boiling onions, cipolline)

2 quarts water with 2 teaspoons salt

1 tablespoon butter

3 tablespoons olive oil

½ teaspoon dried sage, crumbled into powder

½ cup dry white wine

1 teaspoon Poupon-style mustard

1 6-ounce can tuna, drained and flaked

1½ cups long-grain rice

Salt and pepper to taste

Boil the onions in the salted water for ten minutes. Drain, peel, dry, and chop them. In a large, deep skillet, heat butter and oil with sage on moderate heat. Add the wine, mustard, and onions. Stirring, cook on high heat for five minutes. Add flaked tuna, adjust heat to low, and stir for five minutes. Meanwhile, boil rice in slightly salted water for fifteen minutes uncovered. Drain and pour into serving bowl. Cover with onion-tuna sauce. Mix well. Season with salt and pepper. Bring to table and raise a glass of wine to Neptune.

RECOMMENDED WINES:

FIANO DI AVELLINO, TOCAI FRIULANO

Riso e Zucchini Rapido

(QUICK RICE AND ZUCCHINI)

SERVES 4

One evening at my compare *Sandro's house in Reggio Calabria, we were waiting for his wife Clelia to get home from working overtime in her office. Clelia arrived and told us to get out of her kitchen. I sneaked back in, sat quietly in a corner out of her way, and watched as she cooked this dish. Supper was ready in thirty minutes, and it tasted terrific.*

2 tablespoons butter	1 cup boiling hot chicken broth
1 peeled medium onion, diced	2 large eggs, beaten with
1 large clove garlic, crushed	4 teaspoons light cream
4 young small zucchini, washed and diced	4 cups water with teaspoon salt
	1½ cups long-grain rice
Salt and pepper to taste	Pinch oregano
2 tablespoons dry white wine (she used dry vermouth)	

Melt butter in a large saucepan on moderate heat. Add onions. Sauté for eight minutes. Add garlic and sauté two minutes. Add zucchini and stir for two minutes. Season with salt and pepper. Add wine and cook until it evaporates, five minutes. Add boiling hot broth. Stir. Remove from heat. Beat eggs with 2 tablespoons of grated cheese and cream. Add to zucchini and stir vigorously for two minutes. Cook rice in four cups of boiling water for twenty minutes covered. This was actually her first step. She brought water to boil, stirred in rice, adjusted heat to low, and simmered it until done. Dress rice with cooked zucchini. Add pinch of oregano. Sprinkle 2 tablespoons grated cheese and serve.

RECOMMENDED WINES:

VERNACCIA DI SAN GIMIGNANO, FRASCATI

Tortino di Riso

(BAKED RICE CAKE)

SERVES 4

This scrumptious baked rice was served to me as a first course at the home of Geni La Bozzetta Stilo in Reggio Calabria, Italy. I ate two servings and picked at the rest of the meal. It is rich and filling. I serve it as a main course and follow with a simple green salad dressed with fresh lemon juice and extra-virgin olive oil.

4 ounces long-grain rice

3 large eggs, beaten with

3 heaping tablespoons grated
   Pecorino Romano

Salt and pepper to taste

2 tablespoons olive oil

½ peeled large onion, thinly sliced

1 large peeled clove garlic, crushed

1 28-ounce can crushed tomatoes

1 teaspoon dried oregano

1 pound fresh mozzarella cheese,
   thinly sliced

2 tablespoons butter

Plain bread crumbs

Grated Pecorino Romano cheese to
   pass at table

Preheat the oven to 400°. Boil rice in 4 quarts of water salted with 1 teaspoon salt, uncovered. Cook for eighteen minutes, drain and pour into a large bowl in which you have beaten the eggs with the grated cheese. Stir well. Season with salt and pepper. Meanwhile, heat the oil in a large, deep skillet on moderate heat. Sauté onion and garlic for five minutes. Add crushed tomatoes and oregano. Cook uncovered for twenty-five minutes. Set aside. Grease a deep baking dish with butter. Sprinkle with bread crumbs, bottom and sides. Place layer of rice on bottom. Cover with thin slices of mozzarella cheese and a few tablespoons of tomato sauce. Keep on layering rice, cheese, and sauce until all the ingredients are used up. Bake uncovered for twenty minutes. Bring to table immediately and serve. Pass grated cheese.

RECOMMENDED WINES:

NERO D'AVOLA, AGLIANICO

Timballo di Riso Giallo

(RING MOLD OF YELLOW RICE)

SERVES 4

Siena is an indescribably beautiful medieval town famous for its annual Palio (a chaotic horse race) and panforte (a delicious dessert bread of figs, dates, and nuts). I was invited to dinner at San Luigi Restaurant in Monteriggioni, a suburb of Siena, where I experienced this timballo. I say experienced because seeing and tasting it was as close to a religious experience as I ever had with food. It was June 1, 1993, my fifty-sixth birthday, and God gave me a very special birthday gift: this recipe.

1 large scallion, thinly sliced from white bulb to green tops

4 tablespoons butter

10 ounces of veal, cut into small cubes

7 ounces button mushrooms, thinly sliced

1 ounce of dried porcini mushrooms, soaked for ½ hour in warm water, drained, washed, dried on paper towel, and chopped

1 beef bouillon cube, crushed

¼ teaspoon freshly ground black pepper

4 tablespoons whole milk

1 tablespoon heavy cream

1 medium onion, thinly sliced

2 tablespoons olive oil

11 ounces Arborio rice

½ cup dry white wine

1 quart boiling hot beef stock

2 small packages saffron (0.8 gram) dissolved in:

2 tablespoons hot beef stock

2 tablespoons freshly grated Parmesan cheese

¼ cup fresh chopped flat leaf parsley

Preheat oven to 350°. Heat butter in a saucepan on gentle heat and sauté scallion for five minutes. Add veal cubes and cook, stirring often, for ten minutes. Add sliced button mushrooms, crushed bouillon cube, and black pepper. Remove from heat and whisk in milk and cream. Set aside.

In a large saucepan, sauté onion for five minutes in olive oil and 1 tablespoon of butter on moderate heat. Add rice and stir for three minutes. Add wine and cook until evaporated. Add hot broth, cup by cup, until all the liquid is absorbed by the rice (about eighteen minutes), constantly stirring with wooden spoon. During the last minute, add the disolved saffron and grated cheese. Remove from heat and let rest covered for two minutes.

Grease an angel food baking pan with 1 tablespoon of butter. Fill with cooked rice mixture. Press down firmly with wet tablespoon. Dot with remaining tablespoon of butter. Bake for fifteen minutes. Remove from oven and unmold on round, warmed serving dish. Fill the center with mushroom-veal mixture. Garnish with chopped parsley and bring immediately to table. *Paradiso!* (Paradise!)

RECOMMENDED WINES:

BRUNELLO DI MONTALCINO, MORELLINO DI SCANSANO

Ripieno di Riso

(RICE STUFFING)

This rice stuffing can be used to fill bell peppers, tomatoes, cabbage leaves, and even poultry. It is savory and very useful in recipes that require stuffing. The recipe given here is enough to stuff four bell pepper halves or four medium-sized tomatoes. If you need more, simply double or triple the ingredients.

1 teaspoon anchovy paste (comes in a tube like toothpaste—I use Giovanni's Anchovy Paste, Net. Wt. 2 ounces)

1 cup chopped fresh flat leaf parsley

2 cups water with ½ teaspoon salt

1 cup long-grain rice

4 cloves garlic, peeled

12 tablespoons olive oil

¼ cup plain bread crumbs

½ cup grated Pecorino Romano cheese

Wash the chopped parsley well and drain. Put anchovy paste and parsley in bowl of a food processor fitted with a steel blade and pulse for three seconds. Bring water (2 cups) to a boil. Stir in rice and boil for ten minutes. (The rice will finish cooking in the oven inside of whatever you stuff it in.) Drain and pour in bowl. Meanwhile sauté whole garlic cloves in olive oil in a skillet on moderate heat. Cook until golden brown. Remove and discard. (I mash them on a slice of toasted Italian bread and have a tasty snack.) Add anchovy-parsley paste. Adjust heat to low and cook for one minute. Pour over reserved rice. Add bread crumbs and grated cheese. Mix well. It's a savory stuffing.

Insalate di Riso (Rice Salads)

A rice salad can be served as an appetizer, a main course, a side dish, or as a proper salad. The rice is usually long grained, cooked separately in salted water, drained and served hot, at room temperature or cold.

Riso in Insalata con Maionese Verde

(RICE SALAD WITH GREEN MAYONNAISE)

SERVES 4

Varese is a small village close to Lago Maggiore in the northern end of the region of Lombardy. I was invited to dine with relatives of my dear Sicilian friend, Dr. Salvatore Cerniglia. This salad was served as an appetizer to a magnificent meal. It really piqued my appetite.

2 tablespoons small capers

1 small dill pickle

2 ounces pitted green olives

3½-ounce can of tuna packed in olive oil, drained and flaked

11 ounces long-grain rice

1 quart water with 1 teaspoon salt

1 small package frozen spinach cooked to package directions, drained, and squeezed dry

½ cup fresh basil leaves

½ cup chopped fresh flat leaf parsley

Juice of one lemon

1 cup prepared mayonnaise, regular or low-fat

6 tablespoons olive oil

Pinch of salt and pepper

1 small head romaine lettuce, separated, leaves washed and dried

Wash the capers, slice the pickle and slice the the green olives into rounds. Add flaked tuna. Mix all the above in the bottom of a salad bowl. Boil the rice uncovered in the salted water for twenty minutes. Drain and run cold water over it to stop further cooking. Pour into salad bowl and mix with contents on bottom of the bowl. Place spinach, basil, parsley, lemon juice, mayonnaise, oil, and pinches of salt and pepper in a blender. Blend until smooth. Add to contents of salad bowl and toss well. Form a small mountain of the contents in a salad bowl or shallow serving dish lined with lettuce leaves. You are in for a treat!

RECOMMENDED WINES:

ARNEIS, PINOT BIANCO

Insalata di Riso Freddo

(COLD RICE SALAD)

SERVES 6

I tasted a rice salad in Marietta La Bozzetta's home one day and failed to ask for the recipe. I tried to re-create hers. I couldn't forget how good it was. When I returned from Italy a week later, I invented this rice salad. Everyone, me included, judged it to be a winner. So, here is Papa Joe's rice salad. Marietta let me make it the following year—she said, "That's exactly how I make mine."

8 cups water salted with
    1½ teaspoons salt

4 cups long-grain rice

1 large peeled onion, diced

2 6-ounce cans tuna packed in olive
    oil, flaked

3 ribs celery, diced small

2 medium carrots, peeled and diced
    small

1 tablespoon small capers, rinsed in
    cold water and dried with paper
    towel

1 package frozen peas, completely
    thawed

1 14-ounce can artichoke hearts,
    drained and sliced into rings

1 10-ounce jar pitted green olives,
    drained and sliced

Salt and pepper to taste

3 tablespoons red wine vinegar

½ cup olive oil

½ pound mozzarella cheese, diced
    small

½ pound sharp provolone cheese,
    diced small

1 jalapeño pepper with seeds,
    minced

Bring water to boil in a large saucepan. Add rice, stir, and adjust heat to low. Cover and simmer for twenty minutes. Let stand five minutes. While rice is still warm, add all the other ingredients and mix well in your largest bowl. Serve warm, at room temperature, or cold. This is a salad that will have them talking.

RECOMMENDED WINES:

VERMENTINO, INZOLIA/CATARATTO

Insalata Calda di Riso

(HOT RICE SALAD)

SERVES 4

You may serve this colorful and tantalizing salad as an appetizer or as a salad to accompany a main course of meat, poultry, or fish. It's superb.

1½ cups Arborio rice

3 cups water

3½ ounces pancetta or bacon, julienned

2 tablespoons olive oil

1 small peeled onion, minced

4 small heads radicchio, cut into halves and washed

1 ounce pitted black olives

1 6-ounce can corn niblets, drained

1 dash Worcestershire sauce

1 teaspoon freshly ground black pepper

Cook the rice in a large saucepan in three cups of water, uncovered, for eighteen minutes. Pour into colander, drain and run cold water over it to stop its cooking. Leave in colander. Fry the pancetta in a deep skillet in olive oil on moderate heat for five minutes. Add onion, cook another five minutes. Add the radicchio, olives, and corn. Add Worcestershire sauce and black pepper. Cook for five minutes. Add cooked rice and mix well. Heat for five more minutes. Pour into a deep, warm serving bowl and bring to table.

RECOMMENDED WINES:

RIBOLLA GIALLA, TOCAI FRIULANO

Insalata di Riso allo Zafferano

(SAFFRON RICE SALAD)

S E R V E S   4

This is an unusually tasty salad that's perfect for a balmy summer night's supper. Make it in the morning then refrigerate it (covered with plastic wrap of course). Remove it from the refrigerator one hour before supper to allow it to come to room temperature. If your house is air-conditioned, set it out on your porch or picnic table for one hour, no longer. The cream can spoil.

6 tablespoons olive oil	2 cups long-grain rice
3 zucchini, unpeeled and sliced into thin rounds	2 small packages saffron (0.8 gram)
2 red bell peppers, pithed, seeded, and julienned	½ cup boiling hot chicken stock
4 cups water salted with 1 teaspoon salt	½ cup heavy cream
	1 tablespoon cognac
	Salt and pepper to taste

In a large skillet, sauté zucchini rounds in 2 tablespoons of olive oil on moderate heat until lightly browned on both sides. Empty contents of skillet (zucchini and oil) into a bowl. Set aside. In same skillet, sauté julienned red peppers in 2 tablespoons of olive oil on moderate heat until lightly browned. Empty contents into same bowl containing zucchini. Meanwhile, bring water to boil, add rice, adjust heat to low, cover and simmer for twenty minutes. Pour rice into colander and rinse with cold water. Allow to drain well. Pour drained rice into large salad bowl. Dissolve saffron in ½ cup hot chicken broth. Pour into rice and mix well. Beat cream until it begins to thicken. Still beating, add last 2 tablespoons of olive oil and cognac. Beat for two more minutes. Dress salad with this cream dressing. Season with salt and pepper. Add cooked zucchini and peppers with their oil. Stir vigorously. Serve it immediately, or follow suggestions in the introduction to this recipe. This is very special.

RECOMMENDED WINES:

DOLCETTO, PINOT NOIR/NERO

Insalata di Riso con Salsa di Tonno e Capperi

(RICE SALAD WITH TUNA AND CAPER DRESSING)

SERVES 4

This is a very tasty way of preparing a cold rice salad. It is perfect for a warm summer evening's light supper. I was very pleased when I tasted it at the house of Giovanna Maisano (my mother's niece) in Reggio Calabria one sultry August evening.

4 quarts water with 1 teaspoon salt

15 ounces long-grain rice

1 cup fresh flat leaf parsley

¼ small onion

3 tablespoons olive oil

1 tablespoon fresh lemon juice

Salt and pepper to taste

1 6-ounce can tuna packed in olive
   oil, flaked

1 pint plain yogurt

1 hard-boiled egg, quartered

4 heaping tablespoons mayonnaise,
   regular or low-fat

2 tablespoons small capers, drained

½ cup whipped heavy cream (plain
   cream with no sugar)

Bring water to boil. Stir in rice, return to boil, and cook uncovered for twenty minutes. Drain in colander. Rinse with cold water and allow to drain and cool completely in colander. Meanwhile, in bowl of a food processor fitted with a steel blade, process ½ cup of parsley, the onion, olive oil, lemon juice, and salt and pepper until smooth. Empty into a bowl. In the same food processor bowl fitted with steel blade, place tuna, yogurt, hard-boiled egg, mayonnaise and 1 tablespoon of capers and process until smooth. Add half of the reserved onion, oil, and lemon juice dressing. Process for another minute. Transfer to another bowl and hand mix the other half of reserved onion, oil, and lemon dressing. Fold in whipped cream. Mix this dressing with the cold rice in a large bowl. Stir in the remaining tablespoon of capers. Pile onto a serving platter and shape into a little mountain. Either serve immediately or refrigerate, covered with plastic wrap for later use.

RECOMMENDED WINES:

VERMENTINO, FALANGHINA

Dolci (Desserts)

Although Italian regional cuisines offer some delicious cakes, pies, cookies, pastries, and *dolci al cucchiaio* (desserts eaten with a spoon), the favorite Italian way to finish a meal is with fresh fruit in season.

This section contains a few Italian desserts that are all based on rice.

If you wish to serve wine with these desserts, we recommend Martini & Rossi Asti Spumante.

Budino di Riso al Cioccolato
(CHOCOLATE RICE PUDDING)

SERVES 8

This is not like any rice pudding I've ever tasted. It is sumptuously delicious and pleasing to the palate. But it must be made at least four hours in advance. I was visiting the beautiful city of Vicenza and stopped in a confectionery shop to pick up a dessert for my hosts. This pudding caught my eye and I looked no further. My hosts were pleased with my little gift. But when espresso was served, a servant brought out an identical pudding my hostess had made. This is Signora deAngelis' recipe.

1½ quarts whole milk	¼ cup cognac
½ cup sugar	1 cup of sultana raisins, soaked in
Zest of 2 lemons	warm water ½ hour then drained
15 ounces long-grain rice	10 ounces bittersweet chocolate,
3 tablespoons butter	melted in ¼ cup milk on low heat
1 pint heavy cream	in double boiler pot

Before starting the budino, put an empty pudding mold on ice. Boil milk in a saucepan. Add sugar, lemon zest, and rice. Stir on low heat until rice has absorbed all the milk. Remove from heat and stir in butter vigorously. Allow to cool. Whip cream until very stiff. Fold whipped cream into rice pudding. Add cognac and sultana raisins. Stir well. Refrigerate for half hour, then spoon into a very cold pudding mold. Refrigerate for three hours. Unmold onto a serving dish and pour melted hot chocolate over it. Serve immediately.

Budino di Riso alle Mandorle

(ALMOND AND RICE PUDDING)

SERVES 6

When I was in Agrigento, Sicily, early one February and walking the road in the Valley of the Temples, I noticed a sweet fragrance in the air. It was the trees in full blossom lining the roadway. I was informed that they were almond trees. Later that evening, at Kaos, my hotel, this Budino a Mennuli was served for dessert. So from the hotel Kaos in Agrigento, the kitchen staff is saying scialatevi *(enjoy yourselves!).*

1 quart whole milk	1½ ounces raisins, plumped in warm
2 tablespoons sugar	water ½ hour, drained and dried
Grated zest of 1 lemon	4 tablespoons almonds toasted on a
10 ounces long-grain rice	cookie sheet for 10 minutes at
½ pint heavy cream, whipped until	400°, cooled and coarsely
stiff	chopped
1 tablespoon melted butter	1 tablespoon butter
1 shot glass cognac	7 ounces bittersweet chocolate

Place milk, sugar, and grated lemon rind in a saucepan and bring to a boil, stirring constantly. Add rice, lower heat to simmer, and cook, stirring constantly, until the rice has absorbed all the milk. Remove from heat and let cool to room temperature. Fold in whipped cream. Add brandy (cognac), melted butter, raisins, and chopped almonds. Mix well. Grease a bundt pan with butter. Pack in rice pudding. Refrigerate for three hours. Remove from refrigerator and dip pan in hot water ¾ the way up. Invert onto a serving plate. For topping, melt bittersweet chocolate in double boiler or microwave oven. Pour melted chocolate over pudding and serve immediately.

Dolce di Riso e Mandarini

(BAKED RICE AND TANGERINE DESSERT)

SERVES 6

Yes, *this is a complicated recipe that will take approximately 1½ hours of your time. Make it for a special occassion, such as a significant birthday or anniversary. Your loved ones will appreciate you even more.*

1 quart whole milk	9 ounces long-grain rice
1 vanilla pod, cut in half, or	2 tablespoons butter, plus 1
1 teaspoon vanilla extract	tablespoon to grease bundt cake
6 large, juicy tangerines, peeled,	pan
sectioned, seeded, and trimmed	20 sugar cubes
2 shot glasses Grand Marnier	2 tablespoons water
liqueur	1 teaspoon fresh lemon juice
2 tablespoons honey	1 teaspoon butter
2 egg yolks	6 candied cherries
4 tablespoons sugar	6 fresh mint leaves

Preheat oven to 400°. In a saucepan, put the milk and vanilla on to boil. Lower heat and simmer.

Place sections of 4 tangerines into food blender, with the Grand Marnier liqueur and honey. Blend for one minute. In another saucepan, beat the egg yolks with the sugar until creamy and stir in, little by little, the hot milk, discard vanilla pods, and beat with the hand mixer. Turn heat to moderate and cook until the cream becomes thick (about five minutes). Add rice, always stirring. Cook, stirring, for fifteen minutes over moderate heat. Add butter and finally the liquified tangerines. Mix vigorously during the last five minutes of cooking.

Pour into buttered bundt baking pan, being careful to fill it only ¾ up the pan. Place in another pan filled with water ¾ of the way up the bundt pan. Place pans in oven and bake for twenty minutes. Remove from oven and allow to come to room temperature (about fifteen minutes).

Loosen the edges with a butter knife, going all the way down to the bottom of the pan. Invert on a round serving dish.

Now prepare the caramel glaze: Mix 20 sugar cubes, 2 tablespoons of water, 1 teaspoon lemon juice, and 1 teaspoon of butter in a small saucepan on moderate heat until golden brown. Garnish with more tangerine sections. Pour caramel glaze over the pudding. Garnish with 6 candied cherries, indicating where you will slice. Place mint leaves in center. Bring to table, cut, and serve. Magnificent!

Budino di Crema di Riso

(BAKED CREAM OF RICE PUDDING)

SERVES 8

Geni La Bozzetta Stilo served this awesome dessert at a New Year's Eve champagne cocktail party. I was fortunate enough to be there and to get her recipe two days later.

1 quart water with ½ teaspoon salt

18 level tablespoons long-grain rice

1 quart whole milk

1 vanilla pod with beans inside, or
   1 teaspoon vanilla extract

3 tablespoons butter

4 tablespoons sugar

½ cup heavy cream

1 shot glass Amaretto di Saronno
   liqueur

5 egg yolks, beaten

2 tablespoons sultana raisins
   (plumped in tepid water ½ hour,
   drained and dried)

12 Amaretti cookies softened with
   rum and crumbled (Amaretti can
   be mail ordered. Address on page 5)

Pinch of salt

5 egg whites, whipped until they
   form stiff peaks

Preheat oven to 350°. Cook the rice in boiling salted water for four minutes. Bring the milk and vanilla to a boil in another saucepan and add the cooked rice. Cover and simmer on low heat for twenty-five minutes. Pour into blender with butter, sugar, cream, liqueur, and the beaten egg yolks. Blend for a minute until very smooth. Pour into a mixing bowl. Stir in raisins, crumbled cookies soaked in rum, and then fold in stiff egg whites. Smooth into a caramelized baking dish (to caramelize the baking dish, sprinkle 5 tablespoons of sugar on the bottom and stir in 2 tablespoons of water, cook on low heat on top of the stove, stirring constantly with wooden spoon until the sugar becomes a dark brown syrup). Bake in oven placed inside a deeper dish filled with water ¾ the depth of the baking dish containing the *budino*. Bake for forty-five minutes. Remove and allow to cool for twenty minutes, garnish with 4 ounces of grated bittersweet chocolate. Bring to table and serve. You'll never eat ordinary rice pudding again.

Sformato Dolce di Riso alle Nocciole
(BAKED MOLD OF SWEET RICE WITH HAZELNUTS)

SERVES 6

The Sicilians are known throughout Italy as the best pastry chefs and inventors of outrageous desserts. My favorite pastry shop is in Taormina, in Sicily. Its owner, a distinguished and elegant Sicilian, Giuseppe Chemi, and I have become friends. For ten consecutive years he has won the top award for pastries from the Italian National Pastry Association. This recipe won him a special grand award in 1993.

3 heaping tablespoons sultana
    raisins, soaked in tepid water
    ½ hour, drained and dried

10 heaping tablespoons Arborio rice,
    boiled for five minutes, drained

7 tablespoons hazelnuts (filberts),
    toasted, and coarsely chopped

5 tablespoons honey

Grated rind of 1 large orange

1 shot glass of Amaretto di Saronno
    liqueur

2 Amaretti cookies, crushed

6 egg yolks (reserve whites) beaten
    with:

    4 tablespoons sugar and

    2 tablespoons melted butter

½ cup whole milk

¼ cup heavy cream

Pinch of salt

6 reserved egg whites beaten until
    they form stiff peaks

2 tablespoons butter

Plain bread crumbs

8 butter cookies finely chopped (Peak
    Frean brand or Pepperidge Farm)

Preheat oven to 500°. Place the raisins in a mixing bowl. Stir in cooked rice. Add the chopped hazelnuts, honey, grated orange peel, liqueur, and crushed amaretti cookies. Add the beaten egg yolks (containing sugar and melted butter), the milk, and the cream. Stir vigorously. Fold in beaten egg whites with a wooden spoon. Grease a bundt baking pan with 1 tablespoon butter. Dust with bread crumbs. Fill with batter. Level the batter with a wet spatula. Sprinkle with crushed butter cookies and dot with remaining tablespoon of butter. Bake for twenty-five minutes. Lower oven to 350° and place bundt pan on lowest rack for three hours. Unmold on serving plate. (Fill sink with hot water and insert pan ¾ up its side for five minutes to aid in unmolding.) Serve to your guests. This cake can be refrigerated for up to two days covered, then unmolded and served. Congratulations! You've made a gold medal winner.

Budino di Riso al Forno
(BAKED RICE PUDDING)

SERVES 4

It was early in the month of May. I was a guest at the Regina Palace Hotel in the enchanting town of Stresa on the shores of the magnificent Lago Maggiore. I looked out at the shimmering lake surrounded by the Pre-Alpine mountains. It was forty degrees and raining lightly. Soon I walked down to the charming dining room with my traveling companion, Peter Gaglioti of Maywood, New Jersey. The dinner was better than average hotel fare. Near the end of the meal, a waiter dressed in white, rolled out the dessert cart. This rice pudding seemed to call me by name. I answered. It was love at first bite.

1 quart whole milk	Pinch of salt
3½ ounces long-grain rice	2 whole eggs and 2 egg yolks, beaten
3 tablespoons sugar	Shot glass cognac
2 ounces sultana raisins, soaked in warm water ½ hour and drained	½ teaspoon vanilla extract
1 tablespoon candied citron, diced small	2 tablespoons butter
	Plain bread crumbs

Preheat the oven to 350°. Heat milk in a small saucepan to a boil. Add rice. Lower heat to simmer and cook for eight minutes. Add sugar, sultana raisins, 1 tablespoon butter, diced candied citron, and pinch of salt and cook, stirring, another eight minutes. Remove from heat and allow to cool down for ten minutes. Add beaten eggs, cognac, vanilla extract, and mix very well. Grease a bundt baking pan with remaining tablespoon butter and dust with bread crumbs. Bake for thirty minutes. Remove and invert on round serving platter.

Accompany the baked pudding with 3½ ounces apricot jam cooked on gentle heat to loosen, with a half shot glass of cognac, for five minutes. Pour the loosened apricot jam over the top of the pudding. Serve hot.

Coppe di Riso e Ciliege

(RICE AND CHERRY CUPS)

SERVES 6

This is an attractive and delectable dessert that packs a wallop because of the wine and cherry liqueur with which it is made. I tasted this terrific dessert sitting at a table set in the midst of a grove of cherry trees in Enna, Sicily, on a sunny November afternoon with good friends.

10 ounces of very ripe fresh cherries, washed and pitted	3 tablespoons sugar
	Pinch of salt
2 shot glasses of maraschino cherry liqueur	½ teaspoon vanilla extract
	1 cup whole milk
1 tablespoon sugar	2 ounces candied citron, julienned
1½ cups of muscatel wine	6 candied cherries
9 ounces long-grain rice	6 dessert glasses

Place the fresh cherries in a small saucepan with the maraschino liqueur, tablespoon sugar, and wine. Cook on gentle heat for twenty minutes. Drain and reserve liquid. In another saucepan place rice, 3 tablespoons of sugar, pinch of salt, vanilla, milk, and reserved cherry cooking liqueur and stir. Cook on gentle heat, stirring occasionally, until the rice has absorbed almost all the liquid. Mix in the cooked cherries. Distribute into 6 dessert glasses. Garnish around the edges of each cup with julienned candied citron. Place candied cherry in the center of each cup. Refrigerate for two hours, then serve. *Meraviglioso!* (Marvelous!)

Torta di Riso e Banane
(RICE AND BANANA CAKE)

SERVES 4 TO 5

This is a delightful combination of rice and bananas in a not-too-sweet cake. Of course, you should serve Italian espresso in demitasse cups and have a bottle of Anisette or Sambuca on the table.

1 quart whole milk

1 tablespoon granulated sugar

Zest of one lemon (just the outer skin, not the bitter white pith) in one long piece

7 ounces long-grain rice

4 eggs, separated (save egg whites)

4 to 5 Amaretti cookies, crushed

10 ounces of banana, cubed or diced

1 tablespoon candied citron, diced

1 tablespoon butter

Plain bread crumbs

Powdered sugar

Preheat the oven to 350°. Put the milk in a saucepan with the sugar and lemon zest. Put on moderate heat and cook until thick. Remove from heat and discard the lemon zest. Allow to cool.

Beat the egg yolks in a bowl with the sugar until creamy. Add the cooked rice, the crushed cookies, the diced banana, and the candied citron. Mix well. Beat the egg whites until they form stiff peaks. Fold into the rice-banana mixture.

Grease a cake pan with butter. Dust with bread crumbs. Pour in batter. Bake for forty-five minutes. Let cool. Remove from pan. Dust with powdered sugar and serve. Don't forget the espresso and the Sambuca.

Pallottoline di Riso Rosa

(RED RICE BALLS)

SERVES 6

These sweet, red rice balls should be served while they are still hot from deep frying. They should be accompanied by frosty glasses of Asti Spumante or sweet marsala wine.

1 quart whole milk

Zest from 2 oranges—only the outer layer of skin, no white pith

4 tablespoons granulated sugar

2 tablespoons heavy cream

3½ ounces long-grain rice

4 egg yolks

2 shot glasses of Rosolio liqueur, or any other deep, red liqueur, like cherry brandy

1 heaping tablespoon all-purpose flour

Pinch of salt

1 tablespoon vegetable oil

2 tablespoons warm beer

1 teaspoon lukewarm water

2 cups shortening (like Crisco)

Powdered sugar

Bring milk to boil. Add orange zest and sugar. Add cream and rice. Cook on moderate heat, constantly stirring, until it becomes a dense pudding (about thirty-five to forty minutes). Remove from heat. Beat in 2 egg yolks, one by one, and the red liqueur. Pour into bowl of a food processor fitted with a plastic blade and process until smooth (about one minute). Pour into a large, shallow dish and refrigerate for one hour. This forms the above into tiny balls. Then, with slotted spoon remove the tiny balls that have formed. Now prepare the batter separately.

Beat the 2 egg yolks with flour and pinch of salt. Mix in oil, beer, and lukewarm water. Beat until the consistency of cream. Now place the rice balls one by one in the batter. Melt the fat (vegetable shortening) in a deep fryer and bring to high heat. Place a strainer that fits within the dimensions of the deep fryer and drop small amounts of the rice balls into the hot grease. Fry until brown on all sides, remove with strainer and place on paper towels. Continue this frying process until all the rice balls are fried. Pile them on a round dish to form a little mountain. Sprinkle with plenty of powdered sugar. Serve immediately.

Riso Dolce con Pesche ✌

(SWEET RICE WITH PEACHES)

SERVES 6

This wonderful dessert should only be made when peaches are at the height of their season. Please don't try to substitute canned peaches. It would do a great injustice to this recipe and to your family and guests. This recipe was given to me by Claudia La Bozzetta from Reggio Calabria, Italy.

7 ounces long-grain rice	1 tablespoon unsalted butter
½ quart whole milk	3 egg yolks
6 tablespoons sugar	2 tablespoons milk
Pinch of salt	4 large ripe peaches
½ vanilla pod or ½ teaspoon vanilla extract	2 tablespoons sugar
	¼ cup orange juice

Wash the rice in a colander, then place in a saucepan, cover with cold water, and bring to a boil on high heat. Remove from heat. Let stand five minutes, then drain. Run cold water over the rice and drain well. Heat milk, sugar, salt, and vanilla in a saucepan on moderate heat. Add rice and bring to a boil. Stir in butter, lower heat to low, and simmer for fifteen minutes. Remove from heat and loosen the grains with a fork. Then add egg yolks beaten with milk. Stir well. Pour onto a serving dish and, with a palette knife, shape into a cake. Refrigerate for one hour. Immerse the peaches in a large pot of boiling water.

When water returns to a boil, take out the peaches. Peel them, cut into halves, remove the pits, and cut into equal sections. Sprinkle with 2 tablespoons of sugar and orange juice. Refrigerate for two hours. Just before serving the rice pudding, decorate it with the sliced peaches and pour their juice over the top of the pudding, slice, and serve.

Epilogue

It was a bittersweet experience writing this book. Doing the research was a blast, but writing the comments brought back many memories of dear people who have died since I met them. I confess that I don't know a thing about Asian cooking, but I know that there must be thousands of ways of cooking rice in the orient. But my first love is Italy and its cuisines. I guess it's because I'm an Italian.

My fond hope is that you get to know me through my books. Perhaps this short poem will help you understand who Father Giuseppe Orsini really is. It was written by Gaspare Lo Bue in the Sicilian language and it has become my daily prayer before I celebrate Mass.

Accept me as I am
Bread of Life within this Tabernacle
I am here
I am here at your door like a beggar seeking help.
My heart is darkened and all bound up.
It is like a twisted ball of barbed wire,
and I feel it deep within me.
My heart is pinched, afraid, and attacked.
The coldness is beginning to penetrate my bones:
Take me by the hand,
show me the road I must travel.
Wash me with your blood,
forgive me of my sins.
Just one more time I want to eat the Bread of Life

like I used to do when I was innocent so many years ago.
I know I am not worthy
But I . . . if I am truly repentant . . . you will forgive my faults.
Show me your mercy, oh my dear God,
I beg your mercy!
Accept me the way I am.

Thank you, dear reader, for buying this book, and may God bless you with good food, warm friends, and long life!

Father Giuseppe Orsini

Index

almond and rice pudding (*budino di riso alle mandorle*), 141

Alpine rice (*riso dell' Alpino*), 114

Amaretto-flavored risotto (*risotto al profumo d'Amaretto*), 82

Arabian-style rice (*riso degli Arabi*), 102

Arabs, rice cultivation, 1

Arborio rice, 5, 25

artichoke risotto (*risotto con i carciofi*), 72

artichoke risotto with nuts (*risotto con carciofi e noci*), 39

artichoke risotto with peas (*risotto con piselli e carciofi*), 43

avocado sauce, rice with (*riso con salsa di avocado*), 116

baked cream of rice pudding (*budino di crema di riso*), 144

baked mold of sweet rice with hazelnuts (*sformato dolce di riso alle nocciole*), 145

baked rice and tangerine dessert (*dolce di riso e mandarini*), 142–143

baked rice cake (*tortino di riso*), 129

baked rice mold with special sauce (*riso in forma con salsa speciale*), 91–92

baked rice pie (*riso pasticciato al forno*), 99

baked rice pudding (*budino di riso al forno*), 146

baked rice Villa San Giovanni (*riso al forno Villa San Giovanni*), 120–121

baked rice with mushrooms and chicken livers, crusty (*riso gratinato con funghi e fegatini*), 110–111

banana and rice cake (*torta di riso e banane*), 148

Barolo wine risotto (*risotto al Barolo*), 56

Beautiful Helen's risotto (*risotto alla Bella Elena*), 49

beautiful summer risotto (*risotto della bella estate*), 76–77

beef broth (*brodo di manzo*), 5, 6

beet and fava bean risotto (*risotto con fave e bietole*), 33

beggar women's rice (*riso alla pitocca*), 88

boatman's rice (*riso del barcaiolo*), 108

Bolzano risotto (*risotto di Bolzano*), 55

broccoli florets, rice soup with (*minestra di riso con broccoletti*), 19

brussels sprouts risotto (*risotto con cavolini bruxelles*), 83 carbohydrate diets, xiii–xiv

carrot and peas risotto (*risotto con carote e piselli*), 41

cauliflower, rice with eggs and (*riso con uova e cavolfiore*), 109

Cavour, Camillo, 27

Cavour's risotto (*risotto alla Cavour*), 27

chicken, beggar women's rice (*riso alla pitocca*), 88

chicken broth (*brodo di pollo*), 5

chicken livers

crusty baked rice with mushrooms and (*riso gratinato con funghi e fegatini*), 110–111

rice soup with (*minestra di riso con fegatini di pollo*), 16

chocolate rice pudding (*budino di riso al cioccolato*), 140

Clelia's baked risotto (*risotto al forno di Clelia*), 65

cold rice salad (*insalata di riso freddo*), 135

cream of rice and pumpkin soup (*crema di riso e zucca*), 18

crusty baked rice with mushrooms and chicken livers (*riso gratinato con funghi e fegatini*), 110–111

cumin risotto, fresh (*risotto al cumino*), 63

Dalmatian-style risotto (*risotto alla moda Dalamata*), 32

dandelion risotto (*risotto alle radicchielle*), 84

delicate rice soup (*minestra delicata di riso*), 15

desserts (*dolci*), 139–150

almond and rice pudding (*budino di riso alle mandorle*), 141

baked cream of rice pudding (*budino di crema di riso*), 144

baked mold of sweet rice with hazelnuts (*sformato dolce di riso alle nocciole*), 145

baked rice and tangerine dessert (*dolce di riso e mandarini*), 142–143

baked rice pudding (*budino di riso al forno*), 146

chocolate rice pudding (*budino di riso al cioccolato*), 140

red rice balls (*pallottoline di riso rosa*), 149

rice and banana cake (*torta di riso e banane*), 148

rice and cherry cups (*coppe di riso e ciliege*), 147

sweet rice with peaches (*riso dolce con pesche*), 150

deviled risotto (*risotto al diavolicchio*), 53

dice, defined, 6

dolci (desserts). *See* desserts (*dolci*)

dry champagne risotto, mushrooms marinated in (*risotto ai funghi marinati nello supmante*), 36

eggplant

parsley risotto and (*risotto con melanzane e prezzemolo*), 44

red bell pepper risotto with (*risotto con peperoni e melanzane*), 30–31

eggs

green beans with rice and (*riso con uovo e fagiolini*), 93–94

rice mold with (*sformato di riso con le uova*), 119

rice pudding with (*budino di riso con uova*), 103

rice soup with spinach and (*minestra di riso con spinaci e uova*), 22

rice with cauliflower and (*riso con uova e cavolfiore*), 109

Esau's risotto (*risotto Esau*), 78

fava bean and beet risotto (*risotto con fave e bietole*), 33

fennel risotto (*risotto ai finocchi*), 50

fresh cumin risotto (*risotto al cumino*), 63

the glutton's risotto (*risotto del goloso*), 51

Gorgonzola cheese risotto, flavorful (*risotto saporito al Gorgonzola*), 26

gourmet's risotto (*risotto del buongustaio*), 52

green beans and eggs with rice (*riso con uovo e fagiolini*), 93–94

green bean soup, rice and (*minestra di riso e fagiolini*), 20

green mayonnaise, rice salad with (*riso in insalata con maionese verde*), 134

green rice tart (*tortino di riso al verde*), 122

hazelnuts, baked mold of sweet rice with (*sformato dolce di riso alle nocciole*), 145

Helen of Troy, 49

herbs, defined, 6

hot peppers, rice with sweet peppers and (*riso con peperoni e peperoncino*), 113

hot rice salad (*insalata calda di riso*), 136

ingredients and terms, listing of, 9–12

insalate di riso (rice salads). *See* rice salads (*insalate di riso*)

Italy, described, 2–3

julienne, defined, 5

julienne's risotto (*risotto julienne*), 80–81

leek soup, rice and turnip soup with (*minestra di riso, rape, e porri*), 21

lettuce
    rice soup with peas and (*minestra di riso con lattuga e piselli*), 14
    risotto with (*risotto con lattuga*), 35

little yellow mountain of rice (*monticelo giallo di riso*), 90

Malaysian rice (*riso alla Malesiana*), 125

many-flavored rice (*riso ai tanti sapori*), 101

Marietta's baked rice (*riso al forno alla Marietta*), 124

marsala wine and sausage risotto (*risotto con salsiccia e marsala*), 73

Mazzini, Giuseppe, 3

mince, defined, 6

minestre (soups). *See* soups (*minestre*)

mixed greens risotto (*risotto con verdure miste*), 45

monastery risotto (*risotto del convento*), 42

Monday rice (*riso del Lunedi*), 105–106

mountain man's risotto (*risotto del montanaro*), 67–68

mozzarella
    prosciutto and mushroom risotto with (*risotto con funghi, prosciutto, e mozzarella*), 58
    stringy risotto (*risotto filante*), 69

multicolored risotto (*risotto variopinto*), 85

mushrooms
    crusty baked rice with chicken livers and (*riso gratinato con funghi e fegatini*), 110–111
    marinated in dry champagne risotto (*risotto ai funghi marinati nello supmante*), 36
    prosciutto and mozzarella risotto with (*risotto con funghi, prosciutto, e mozzarella*), 58
    risotto my way (*risotto con funghi alla mia maniera*), 64
    woodman's risotto (*risotto del boscaiolo*), 34

the nanny's risotto (*risotto della tata*), 66

Neptune's rice (*riso Nettuno*), 127

Norcia-style baked rice (*riso al forno del Norcino*), 117

Northern Italy, 1

nutmeg, rice and pumpkin soup perfumed with (*riso e zucca al profumo di noce moscata*), 24

Oktoberfest risotto (*risotto Oktoberfest*), 79

onion sauce, rice with (*riso con salsa di cipolle*), 115

pan-fried rice with prosciutto and peas (*riso in padella con prosciutto e piselli*), 97

Parmesan cheese, 5

parsley, defined, 6

parsley and eggplant risotto (*risotto con melanzane e prezzemolo*), 44

pea and rice soup (*risi e bisi*), 23

peaches, sweet rice with (*riso dolce con pesche*), 150

peas

    artichoke risotto with (*risotto con piselli e carciofi*), 43

    carrot risotto with (*risotto con carote e piselli*), 41

    pan-fried rice with prosciutto and (*riso in padella con prosciutto e piselli*), 97

    rice soup with lettuce and (*minestra di riso con lattuga e piselli*), 14

    spinach risotto with (*risotto con piselli e spinaci*), 54

peasant lady's rice cake (*tortino di riso alla rustica*), 95–96

peasant lady's risotto (*risotto alla rustica*), 28

Pecorino Romano cheese, 5

peppers

    rice with sweet and hot peppers (*riso con peperoni e peperoncino*), 113

    yellow risotto with (*risotto giallo con peperoni*), 29

Philbin, Regis, xi, 1–2

pioneer-style rice (*riso alla moda del pioniere*), 100

police spy's risotto (*risotto dello sbirro*), 71

poor man's risotto (*risotto povero*), 74

potato and zucchine risotto (*risotto con patate e zucchine*), 75

prosciutto

    mushroom, and mozzarella risotto (*risotto con funghi, prosciutto, e mozzarella*), 58

    pan-fried rice with peas and (*riso in padella con prosciutto e piselli*), 97

pumpkin soup

    cream of rice and (*crema di riso e zucca*), 18

    with rice, perfumed with nutmeg (*riso e zucca al profumo di noce moscata*), 24

quick rice and zucchini (*riso e zucchini rapido*), 128

radicchio risotto (*risotto al radicchio*), 40

red bell pepper risotto (*risotto ai peperoni*), 60

red bell pepper risotto with eggplant (*risotto con peperoni e melanzane*), 30–31

red cabbage, rice soup with (*minestra di riso con cavolo rosso*), 16

red rice balls (*pallottoline di riso rosa*), 149

the reverend's risotto (*risotto del reverendo*), 57

rice

    turnip and leek soup (*minestra di riso, rape, e porri*), 21

    types of, 5

rice and banana cake (*torta di riso e banane*), 148

rice and cherry cups (*coppe di riso e ciliege*), 147

rice and green bean soup (*minestra di riso e fagiolini*), 20

rice and pea soup (*risi e bisi*), 23

rice and pumpkin soup perfumed with nutmeg (*riso e zucca al profumo di noce moscata*), 24

rice and tripe (*riso e trippa*), 104

rice croquettes (*arancini*), 1

rice dishes (*risi*), 87–132

    Alpine rice (*riso dell' Alpino*), 114

Arabian-style rice (*riso degli Arabi*), 102

baked rice cake (*tortino di riso*), 129

baked rice mold with special sauce (*riso in forma con salsa speciale*), 91–92

baked rice pie (*riso pasticciato al forno*), 99

baked rice Villa San Giovanni (*riso al forno Villa San Giovanni*), 120–121

beggar women's rice (*riso alla pitocca*), 88

boatman's rice (*riso del barcaiolo*), 108

crusty baked rice with mushrooms and chicken livers (*riso gratinato con funghi e fegatini*), 110–111

generally, 87

green rice tart (*tortino di riso al verde*), 122

little yellow mountain of rice (*monticelo giallo di riso*), 90

Malaysian rice (*riso alla Malesiana*), 125

many-flavored rice (*riso ai tanti sapori*), 101

Marietta's baked rice (*riso al forno alla Marietta*), 124

Monday rice (*riso del Lunedi*), 105–106

Neptune's rice (*riso Nettuno*), 127

Norcia-style baked rice (*riso al forno del Norcino*), 117

pan-fried rice with prosciutto and peas (*riso in padella con prosciutto e piselli*), 97

peasant lady's rice cake (*tortino di riso alla rustica*), 95–96

pioneer-style rice (*riso alla moda del pioniere*), 100

quick rice and zucchini (*riso e zucchini rapido*), 128

rice and tripe (*riso e trippa*), 104

rice mold with eggs (*sformato di riso con le uova*), 119

rice of the sun king (*riso del re sole*), 112

rice pudding with eggs (*budino di riso con uova*), 103

rice stuffing (*ripieno di riso*), 132

rice with avocado sauce (*riso con salsa di avocado*), 116

rice with egg and cauliflower (*riso con uova e cavolfiore*), 109

rice with egg and green beans (*riso con uovo e fagiolini*), 93–94

rice with onion sauce (*riso con salsa di cipolle*), 115

rice with saffron sauce (*riso con salsa allo zafferano*), 107

rice with savoy cabbage and sausages (*riso e verze con salsicci*), 126

rice with slivered almonds (*riso con filetti di mandorle*), 89

rice with sweet and hot peppers (*riso con peperoni e peperoncino*), 113

ring mold of yellow rice (*timballo di riso giallo*), 130–131

San Remo rice (*riso San Remo*), 118

Swiss cheese rice (*riso all' Emmental*), 98

tomato sauced rice (*riso al pomodoro*), 123

rice mold with eggs (*sformato di riso con le uova*), 119

rice of the sun king (*riso del re sole*), 112

rice pudding

almond (*budino di riso alle mandorle*), 141

baked (*budino di riso al forno*), 146

baked cream of (*budino di crema di riso*), 144

chocolate (*budino di riso al cioccolato*), 140

with eggs (*budino di riso con uova*), 103

rice salads (*insalate di riso*), 133–138

cold rice salad (*insalata di riso freddo*), 135

hot rice salad (*insalata calda di riso*), 136

rice salad with green mayonnaise (*riso in insalata con maionese verde*), 134

rice salad with tuna and caper dressing (*insalata di riso con salsa di tonno e capperi*), 138

saffron rice salad (*insalata di riso allo zafferano*), 137

versatility of, 133

rice salad with green mayonnaise (*riso in insalata con maionese verde*), 134

rice soup, delicate (*minestra delicata di riso*), 15

rice soup with broccoli florets (*minestra di riso con broccoletti*), 19

rice soup with chicken livers (*minestra di riso con fegatini di pollo*), 16

rice soup with lettuce and peas (*minestra di riso con lattuga e piselli*), 14

rice soup with red cabbage (*minestra di riso con cavolo rosso*), 16

rice soup with spinach and eggs (*minestra di riso con spinaci e uova*), 22

rice stuffing (*ripieno di riso*), 132

rice with avocado sauce (*riso con salsa di avocado*), 116

rice with egg and cauliflower (*riso con uova e cavolfiore*), 109

rice with egg and green beans (*riso con uovo e fagiolini*), 93–94

rice with onion sauce (*riso con salsa di cipolle*), 115

rice with saffron sauce (*riso con salsa allo zafferano*), 107

rice with savoy cabbage and sausages (*riso e verze con salsicci*), 126

rice with slivered almonds (*riso con filetti di mandorle*), 89

rice with sweet and hot peppers (*riso con peperoni e peperoncino*), 113

ring mold of yellow rice (*timballo di riso giallo*), 130–131

risi (rice dishes). *See* rice dishes (*risi*)

risotti (risottos). *See* risottos (*risotti*)

risotto Calabrese, 1–2

risotto from Brindisi (*risotto Brindisano*), 59

risotto in a green field (*risotto in campo verde*), 61

risottos (*risotti*), 25–85

    Amaretto-flavored risotto (*risotto al profumo d'Amaretto*), 82

artichoke and nut risotto (*risotto con carciofi e noci*), 39

artichoke risotto (*risotto con i carciofi*), 72

Barolo wine risotto (*risotto al Barolo*), 56

basics of, 1–2, 25

Beautiful Helen's risotto (*risotto alla Bella Elena*), 49

beautiful summer risotto (*risotto della bella estate*), 76–77

Bolzano risotto (*risotto di Bolzano*), 55

brussels sprouts risotto (*risotto con cavolini bruxelles*), 83

carrot and peas risotto (*risotto con carote e piselli*), 41

Cavour's risotto (*risotto alla Cavour*), 27

Clelia's baked risotto (*risotto al forno di Clelia*), 65

Dalmatian-style risotto (*risotto alla moda Dalamata*), 32

dandelion risotto (*risotto alle radicchielle*), 84

deviled risotto (*risotto al diavolicchio*), 53

eggplant and parsley risotto (*risotto con melanzane e prezzemolo*), 44

Esau's risotto (*risotto Esau*), 78

fava bean and beet risotto (*risotto con fave e bietole*), 33

fennel risotto (*risotto ai finocchi*), 50

fresh cumin risotto (*risotto al cumino*), 63

the glutton's risotto (*risotto del goloso*), 51

Gorgonzola cheese risotto, flavorful (*risotto saporito al Gorgonzola*), 26

gourmet's risotto (*risotto del buongustaio*), 52

julienne's risotto (*risotto julienne*), 80–81

mixed greens risotto (*risotto con verdure miste*), 45

monastery risotto (*risotto del convento*), 42

mountain man's risotto (*risotto del montanaro*), 67–68

multicolored risotto (*risotto variopinto*), 85

mushroom, prosciutto, and mozzarella risotto (*risotto con funghi, prosciutto, e mozzarella*), 58

mushroom risotto my way (*risotto con funghi alla mia maniera*), 64

mushrooms marinated in dry champagne risotto (*risotto ai funghi marinati nello supmante*), 36

the nanny's risotto (*risotto della tata*), 66

Oktoberfest risotto (*risotto Oktoberfest*), 79

peas and artichoke risotto (*risotto con piselli e carciofi*), 43

peas and spinach risotto (*risotto con piselli e spinaci*), 54

peasant lady's risotto (*risotto alla rustica*), 28

police spy's risotto (*risotto dello sbirro*), 71

poor man's risotto (*risotto povero*), 74

potato and zucchine risotto (*risotto con patate e zucchine*), 75

radicchio risotto (*risotto al radicchio*), 40

red bell pepper and eggplant risotto (*risotto con peperoni e melanzane*), 30–31

red bell pepper risotto (*risotto ai peperoni*), 60

the reverend's risotto (*risotto del reverendo*), 57

risotto from Brindisi (*risotto Brindisano*), 59

risotto in a green field (*risotto in campo verde*), 61

risotto with lettuce (*risotto con lattuga*), 35

sausage and marsala wine risotto (*risotto con salsiccia e marsala*), 73

small-squid risotto (*risotto con calamaretti*), 70

springtime risotto (*risotto primavera*), 37

stringy risotto (*risotto filante*), 69

three-cheese risotto (*risotto ai tre formaggi*), 62

tuna-flavored risotto (*risotto al sapore di tonno*), 48

Turkish-style risotto (*risotto alla moda Turchese*), 46–47

veal kidney risotto (*risotto con rognoni*), 38

woodman's risotto (*risotto del boscaiolo*), 34

yellow risotto with peppers (*risotto giallo con peperoni*), 29

risotto with lettuce (*risotto con lattuga*), 35

saffron rice salad (*insalata di riso allo zafferano*), 137

saffron sauce, rice with (*riso con salsa allo zafferano*), 107

salads. *See* rice salads (*insalate di riso*)

San Marino, republic of, 3

San Remo rice (*riso San Remo*), 118

Sardinia, 2

Saurini, Alfredo, xiv

sausage

marsala wine risotto with (*risotto con salsiccia e marsala*), 73

rice and savoy cabbage with (*riso e verze con salsicci*), 126

savoy cabbage with rice and sausages (*riso e verze con salsicci*), 126

Sicily, 1, 2

Simone, Don, xiii–xiv

slivered almonds with rice (*riso con filetti di mandorle*), 89

small-squid risotto (*risotto con calamaretti*), 70

soups (*minestre*), 13–24

cream of rice and pumpkin soup (*crema di riso e zucca*), 18

delicate rice soup (*minestra delicata di riso*), 15

rice, turnip and leek soup (*minestra di riso, rape, e porri*), 21

rice and green bean soup (*minestra di riso e fagiolini*), 20

soups *(continued)*

rice and pea soup *(risi e bisi)*, 23

rice and pumpkin soup perfumed with
nutmeg *(riso e zucca al profumo di noce
moscata)*, 24

rice soup with broccoli florets *(minestra
di riso con broccoletti)*, 19

rice soup with chicken livers *(minestra di
riso con fegatini di pollo)*, 16

rice soup with lettuce and peas *(minestra
di riso con lattuga e piselli)*, 14

rice soup with red cabbage *(minestra di
riso con cavolo rosso)*, 16

rice soup with spinach and eggs *(minestra
di riso con spinaci e uova)*, 22

spinach

and peas risotto *(risotto con piselli e
spinaci)*, 54

rice soup with eggs and *(minestra di riso
con spinaci e uova)*, 22

springtime risotto *(risotto primavera)*, 37

squid risotto *(risotto con calamaretti)*, 70

stocks, 5

stringy risotto *(risotto filante)*, 69

summer risotto, beautiful *(risotto della bella
estate)*, 76–77

sweet peppers, rice with hot peppers and
(riso con peperoni e peperoncino), 113

sweet rice with peaches *(riso dolce con pesche)*,
150

Swiss cheese rice *(riso all' Emmental)*, 98

tangerine, baked rice and tangerine dessert
(dolce di riso e mandarini), 142–143

three-cheese risotto *(risotto ai tre formaggi)*,
62

tomato sauced rice *(riso al pomodoro)*, 123

tripe and rice *(riso e trippa)*, 104

tuna and caper dressing, rice salad with
*(insalata di riso con salsa di tonno e
capperi)*, 138

tuna-flavored risotto *(risotto al sapore di
tonno)*, 48

Turkish-style risotto *(risotto alla moda
Turchese)*, 46–47

turnip soup, rice and leek soup with
(minestra di riso, rape, e porri), 21

Vatican City state, 3

veal kidney risotto *(risotto con rognoni)*, 38

walnuts, artichoke and nut risotto *(risotto
con carciofi e noci)*, 39

wine, centrality of, xiv

woodman's risotto *(risotto del boscaiolo)*, 34

yellow risotto with peppers *(risotto giallo con
peperoni)*, 29

zucchini

potato risotto and *(risotto con patate e
zucchine)*, 75

quick rice and *(riso e zucchini rapido)*, 128